SPONSORSHIP IN THE UNITED STATES CONTEXT: THEORY AND PRAXIS

EDITED BY

ROSEMARY SMITH, SC

WARREN BROWN, OMI

NANCY REYNOLDS, SP

CANON LAW SOCIETY OF AMERICA

ISBN: 1-932208-14-3
SAN: 237-6296

Canon Law Society of America
Office of the Executive Coordinator
108 North Payne Street, Suite C
Alexandria, VA 22314-2906

Table of Contents

FOREWORD

The Canon Law Society of America (CLSA) serves the Church in the United States and, by extension, other parts of the world by its scholarly research, by resourcing the People of God, clergy and laity alike, and by advocating for justice, ecumenism and good order within the Church.

In recent decades many of the ministries of the Church in the United States (e.g., education, healthcare, social services outreach) have experienced remarkable shifts in the manner in which they are delivered, animated and overseen. These ministries are generally referred to as 'sponsored works' and frequently, although not exclusively, they have traditionally related to one or several of the hundreds of religious institutes, secular institutes and societies of apostolic life present in this country. As these ministries face new horizons and new challenges, questions repeatedly surface regarding how best to facilitate their successful transition into the future; specifically questions arise regarding what are the preferred civil law and canon law structures, as well as how these two disciplines interface. It has become evident to many observers that some extended reflection from a canonical perspective might benefit the whole community of believers.

The mandate given by the CLSA's Board of Governors (BOG) in 2002 to the CLSA Committee on Consecrated Life and Societies of Apostolic Life (Committee) included identifying and researching topics with significant ramification for institutes of consecrated life and societies of apostolic life. After some preliminary 'market testing' among selected members of the CLSA and other persons knowledgeable of religious institutes,[1] their members and ministries, the Committee proposed to the BOG of the CLSA a research project on sponsorship. This project was envisioned to include scholarly research and

[1] Hereafter unless otherwise indicated the terms 'religious institutes' and 'religious' are used generically to designate religious institutes, secular institutes and societies of apostolic life and the members of these groups.

to eventuate in a publication which would be of service to a wide spectrum of the Church in the United States.

In spring 2004 the BOG approved the Committee's proposed project on sponsorship and the Committee then began refining and fleshing out the project. An invitation-only symposium was designed whereby a group of authors experienced in different facets of the subject area would prepare papers on a particular designated topic and then gather for discussion and exchange. In spring 2005, prior to the symposium itself, the prepared papers were distributed to each participant of the symposium for review. On June 10-12, 2005 the Committee and the authors met together at the Catholic University of America's Theological College in Washington, DC during which time the papers were probed and critiqued through lively discussion and in an atmosphere of collegial learning. In light of this exchange the original authors were then asked to revise their papers and resubmit them by September 1, 2005.

In the course of the symposium gathering and in order to facilitate the discussion, participants agreed to a common definition of sponsorship, a definition which drew heavily on that developed previously by the Catholic Health Association.[2] The agreed upon definition for the CLSA project was:

> *Sponsorship of an apostolate or ministry is a formal relationship between a recognized Catholic organization and a legally formed entity, entered into for the sake of promoting and sustaining the Church's mission in the world.*

Although this definition was not a perfect fit for all of the authors, it served as a starting point or common ground from which and against which individual authors could develop their topic and perspectives.

Upon receipt of the revised papers the editing process then ensued. In early 2006, with the editing process completed, the project was submitted to the Office of the CLSA's Executive Coordinator for final review and publication.

The members of the Committee which shepherded this project wish to thank the many people who contributed to this project. In addition to the authors who gifted the project with their expertise, wisdom, time and personal interest, the Committee is grateful to many others: Sister Sharon Euart, RSM, who, as Vice-President of the CLSA, assisted in the early stages of the project's formulation; Sister Sharon Holland, IHM, an official of the Vatican Congregation for Institutes of Consecrated Life and Societies of Apostolic

[2] Bouchard, Charles E., OP, Gottemoeller, et. al, "Toward a Theology of Catholic Health Care Sponsorship—A Work in Progress," in *Sponsorship: Resources for Sponsors* (St. Louis: The Catholic Health Association of the United States, 2005), 9.

Life, who offered both encouragement and a generous introduction; Brian Mandigo, facilities manager at The Catholic University of America's Theological College, who went out of his way to accommodate the Symposium gathering in June 2005; Sister Anne Diehl, CSJ, who shared her extraordinary secretarial skills during the Symposium gathering itself; and, finally, those who so graciously hosted the Committee during its extended working sessions at the Oblate Renewal Center and Oblate School of Theology in San Antonio, Texas; the Motherhouse of the Sisters of Providence of St. Mary-of-the-Woods, Indiana, and the Bon Secours Richmond Health System in Richmond, Virginia. Without these many extra kindnesses the project would have been considerably more difficult.

Rosemary Smith, SC
Warren Brown, OMI
Nancy Reynolds, SP

March 25, 2006

INTRODUCTION

"When All Is Said and Done..."

When all is said and done, what is sponsorship? For so long we have been accustomed to Catholic schools, hospitals and other apostolic works of the Church being in the hands of a diocese or a religious congregation, that no need was felt to put a name on the relationship, much less to define it. Now many things have changed.

What is made clear by this CLSA Symposium on Sponsorship is, of course, that not all has been said and done. This is an indication, not of the Symposium's failure, but of its success. Rather than a debate toward a final definition, participants moved the question forward through research into historical realities and shifting contemporary sociological and ecclesial contexts.

Of no lesser importance, they raised and focused issues and questions. What is at stake is not simply the canonical or theological meaning of a word, but rather the future of apostolic works fundamental to the Church's mission. How the reality labeled "sponsorship" is structured directly impacts the future *catholicity* — in name and in fact — of education, health care, and social services which have traditionally been exercised in the name of the Church.

Experts in both canon law and American civil law query: Is it wise to use a word which has neither a canonical nor a civil law definition when seeking to establish a relationship in which rights and responsibilities require clear juridic expression and protection? On the other hand, Can technical legal language adequately embody and secure ministries dependent on theological and ethical principles?

The present studies remind us that this topic is not really new. In the decades following Vatican Council II ecclesial ministries, long in the hands of religious, began to experience the impact of changing times. As the available number of religious declined and the teachings of the Council were heard, laity came to be numbered increasingly among the key protagonists in Catholic institutions of health care and of higher education. Educational institutions experimented with an expanded presence of lay trustees on their boards. In the face of increased cost, complexity and competition in the field of health care, civilly recognized Catholic systems replaced stand alone institutions.

As the implications of such actions become more evident, the famous McGrath-Maida debate ensued. Canonists opined on whether separate civil incorporation of apostolates involved the alienation of ecclesiastical property. A solution, at least for the time, was found in the formulation of powers, "reserved" to religious government, which could be protected in civil documents of incorporation. Thus the Catholic identity of the works could be preserved and the properties remain ecclesiastical goods, canonically pertaining to the stable patrimony of the religious institute.

But the socio-ecclesial context within which these works are carried on has continued to change. Particularly in the corporate structures of health care, realities have pushed toward a further evolution. This, in turn, has suggested new canonical structures to parallel the realigned civil systems of earlier decades. Public juridic personality in the canonical sphere has been accorded certain civil systems, with the reserve powers passing into the hands of appointed lay or religious members, rather than remaining in those of religious superiors and councils. In the ongoing debate over these "new" public juridic persons, discussion covers a broad range of issues. These include vigilance over Catholic identity, the administration of ecclesiastical goods, charism, civil and canonical terminology, the readiness of lay executives to maintain an orientation of ministry over business, and competency for the concession of juridic personality. Inter-congregational structures of collaboration have added to the complexity of the matter, precipitating, among others, the question of whether catholicity is to take precedence over specific charisms.

Experimentation with new structures had come first in the field of Catholic higher education. Today, however, the primary locus of discussion is among Catholic health care providers. The concrete factors are quite diverse. Symposium papers explore a diversity of models which either exist or conceivably might prove useful in the future.

Among the issues which weave through the considerations are the relationship between sponsorship and ownership and the relationship between sponsorship and governance. In this context emerge varying opinions on the relative importance of religious being a presence and/or influence in the institutions they founded, or having control of them. To a certain extent these arguments gravitate around the central issue of how the Catholic identity of an institutional ministry can be maintained into the future. What juridic structures best protect faith and ethical values, a sense of mission, the social teachings of the Church regarding justice and concern for the poor, and collaboration with the laity? What formative programs can be offered to permeate institutions at all levels with the sense of mission and a particular evangelical spirit?

The experts gathered at the CLSA Symposium represented canon law, civil law, and the ministries in question. They moved the discussion forward without pretending to say the final word. From time to time, as an undergirding for juridic considerations, the theme of communio was highlighted.

When all is said and done, the topic of sponsorship is about ecclesial ministry, and the goal is to protect it into the future as service rendered in the name of the Church.

Sharon Holland, IHM
January 2006

CHAPTER ONE

Reflections on Sponsorship: One Congregation's Perspective

HELEN MARIE BURNS, RSM

Where we stand determines to a great extent what we see and what we understand. Multiple, interactive relationships influence the experience of any particular component or aspect of one's life. An article in *Catholic Health Progress* introduces the concept of gestalt to explain this phenomenon in relation to the experience and understanding of sponsorship: "how one experiences and (consequently) describes, understands, and values 'sponsorship' is significantly affected by where one stands in the 'field' or the gestalt that is Catholic health care."[1] By way of introduction, then, I will name the standpoint of the experience I bring to the subject of sponsorship of institutional works and describe the time frame I intend to use as the base of my reflection on this experience.

Experience

While I have a doctoral degree in the history of religion and religious thought in the United States, my expertise in the question of sponsorship comes primarily from personal reflection on my experience as a member of a religious congregation of women heavily involved in institutional ministry and as a congregational leader for twenty-some years in that same congregation.[2]

[1] Michael D. Place, "Toward a Theology of Sponsorship," in *Water Will Find a Way: The Ministry of Sponsorship Will Find a Way* (St. Louis, MO: Catholic Health Association, 2005), 19.

[2] The Institute of the Sisters of Mercy of the Americas is an international community of 4617 members dedicated to the works of mercy. Members serve in North, South and Central America, the Caribbean, Guam and the Philippines. The 25 regional communities of the Institute sponsor or co-sponsor seven major national healthcare systems, 18 colleges and universities, 40-some secondary schools, several elementary and preschools, and affordable housing developments.

The Institute of the Sisters of Mercy, Regional Community of Detroit (Farmington Hills, MI) is a participating entity of a newly established public juridic person, Catholic Health Ministries, that sponsors a multi-institutional and multi-congregational health system; sponsors a high school (enrollment of approximately 1000 young women) and a Mercy Education Project (tutoring and mentoring activities); and co-sponsors a university and a middle school for at-risk young women in the city of Detroit.

Leadership in the Sisters of Mercy has provided me many opportunities to serve in governance roles vis-à-vis our educational and health care ministries. In addition, I have had the opportunity to participate in several forums designed to explore various understandings of sponsorship and to design effective sponsorship structures. My own participation in the Leadership Conference of Women Religious also added breadth and depth to my awareness of the concerns and opportunities facing religious congregations in the last decades of the twentieth century regarding the long-term institutional ministries for which they felt responsible and accountable.

Time Frame

These last decades of the twentieth century, 1970 through 2000, provide the general time frame for my reflections on sponsorship. They are the years in which I have been an actor and an observer of the phenomenon of sponsorship in the U. S. Catholic Church. They are also the decades in which the concept, processes and structures of sponsorship have become most defined, at least in the experience of Roman Catholicism in the United States. Concurrently, these decades saw the proclamations and structural shifts occasioned by the insights and inspiration of Vatican II, the global involvement and doctrinal containment of John Paul II, and the growth of fundamentalist and conservative movements within and without Roman Catholicism.

There is a critical link between institutions of service in the name of the Church and the Church's self-understanding. There is also a critical link between the charismatic elements of the Church (partially represented by religious congregations of women and men) and the Church's self-understanding. This broader Church context profoundly affects the relationship between religious congregations and their institutional ministry. In addition, the specific history of a religious congregation and its institutional ministry and the specific history of Catholicism in the United States also profoundly affect this relationship and, hence, any on-going discussion of sponsorship.

I will, then, approach the task of reflection on the recent history of sponsorship in three parts: some brief observations regarding the story of U.S. Catholicism; a brief discussion of the context for understanding the relationship between religious congregations and their institutional ministry; and a case study approach to my experience and understanding of sponsorship in the closing decades of the twentieth century.

Observations on the story of U.S. Catholicism

U.S. Catholicism predates the founding of the country and began with the exploration and expansion of rising nation-states in Europe, particularly the Catholic countries of Spain and France. In the fifteenth and sixteenth centuries Spanish and French missionaries traversed this country along with Spanish soldiers and explorers and French soldiers and trappers. Then, colonization efforts were introduced in the seventeenth and eighteenth centuries by Dutch and English settlers, most of whom were members of Protestant reformation churches. This was a time of distinctions and boundaries, not only among and between colonizing efforts, but also among and between church denominations. Both Roman Catholic and Protestant peoples operated out of an ecclesiology that emphasized its claim to be "the one, true Church intended by Jesus Christ." A siege mentality among and between these various faith communities, stemming from the Council of Trent and the Protestant Reformation, assumed enmity and adversarial relationships vis-à-vis one another. By the late eighteenth and early nineteenth century, Roman Catholicism held minority status in a culture predominantly Protestant and, often, anti-Catholic.

During the nineteenth century, however, large numbers of Catholic immigrant peoples from northern and southern Europe arrived in the United States and the Roman Catholic Church become more visible in the landscape of U.S. culture. This very visibility fueled both anti-American accusations and anti-Catholic sentiments as large numbers of Roman Catholic peoples were poor, unfamiliar with U. S. ways, and isolated by language, customs, and educational and/or social status. The Catholic Church externally struggled for acceptance and respectability and, internally, for continuity and survival. Institutional ministries of diocesan and congregational origin often served as a safe haven for church members and a symbol of strength to sectarian observers. Not every church-related institutional work within U.S. Catholic history was a response to unmet human needs. Institutions of health care, education, and social service were also instruments in the struggle to gain respectability, maintain continuity, and ensure survival. The impetus for many a school, hospital, social service center differs greatly depending on the historical time/place of its founding and the particular vision that occasioned its beginning.

The story of the various institutional works of mercy within the history of the U.S. Church is a complex rather than a simple story. To the extent that these institutional works were connected to the energy and tradition of a religious congregation of women or men, the works participate in the purpose and vision of that particular tradition. Their early institutional culture was shaped by persons dedicated primarily to a congregational mission of which the specific institutional work was a piece, a means to an end. To the extent that these institutional works were connected to the energy of a developing ecclesiastical entity, the works participated in the effort to create stability within a faith community and to establish credibility within the larger social order. This early institutional culture was shaped by its relationship to the most proximate members of that faith community and the most influential members of the larger social order. Sponsorship as a term and an experience within religious congregations of women and men was non-existent for much of that history, but grew out of its multidimensional purpose and vision. That is, sponsorship as a term and an experience grew out of institutional works as a reflection of and instrument for congregational identity and as a reflection of and instrument for ecclesiastical identity. The current experience and understanding of sponsorship cannot afford to neglect a careful reading of the longer history of institutional ministry in the U.S. Catholic Church.

Relationship Between Religious Congregations and Their Institutional Ministry

A piece of the complex story of sponsorship can be found in the historical relationship between a religious congregation and its institutional ministry. This relationship is similar to the relationship of a diocese to its institutional ministry, but is dissimilar in at least one significant element. While both a diocese and a religious congregation consider their institutional ministry an expression of the works of mercy at the heart of the Gospel message, religious congregations often offer a nuance to the spirit of their institutions that centers the energy of this service in a particular focus and pattern of service that extends over time and space and reflects the particular story and tradition of their religious congregation. The Gospel message of service is embodied in trans-diocesan personalities, approaches, spiritualities, customs, and celebrations. This difference is subtle, fragile, and often contingent upon the immediacy of a specific congregation's presence to its ministry. The *Constitutions* of the Sisters of Mercy expresses the nature of the relationship in this manner:

> As Sisters of Mercy we sponsor institutions to address our enduring concerns and to witness to Christ's mission. Within these institutions we, together with our co-workers and those we serve, endeavor *to model mercy and justice and to promote systemic change...*[3]

Many persons would like to think that there is an earlier history in which the link between the particular story and tradition of a religious congregation and its focus and pattern of service in the daily care of persons who were poor, sick, or ignorant was direct, clear, and quite distinguishable from other humane efforts to offer similar care. In that world, the formative influence of women and men religious was immediate and visible. Members of religious congregations saw themselves and were seen by others as centers of energy offering both visibility and stability to the teaching, healing, and consoling ministry of the Catholic Church. The past presents, however, a more complicated picture. Often institutions of health care, education and social service were founded by a particular religious congregation as a spontaneous response to social needs. Often, however, these institutions were founded in response to the invitation of local citizenry who may or may not have been Catholic, or were founded by the citizenry and eventually turned over to a religious congregation. Often, too, these institutions were founded in response to developing ecclesiastical, pastoral, and sectarian needs. On occasion, an institution was founded solely on the basis of denominational competition. In many instances, all three factors drove the foundation.

For the Catholic Church in the United States, the nineteenth-century proliferation of apostolic congregations of women and men religious provided personnel and resources to assist in meeting the challenges of immigration, industrialization and westward expansion.[4] The link to the particular story and

[3] *Constitutions*, Sisters of Mercy #5 (emphasis added).

[4] The contributions of religious congregations of women and men to the growth and development of the U.S. Catholic Church is well documented by several historians of U.S. Catholicism (e.g., Patrick Carey, Jay Dolan, John Tracy Ellis, Mary Ewens, and Delores Liptak).

tradition of a religious congregation and its focus and pattern of service in the past, as is true today and will be true in the future, depended on creative, committed persons who responded to persons in need with competence and compassion, aware of the congregational vision and risking the compromises inherent in all human endeavors. In the past, those competent and compassionate persons were most often members of the founding religious congregation. They worked, therefore, within a life context influenced by the story and tradition of that religious congregation. That story and tradition within the larger story and tradition of U.S. Catholicism created its own lexicon and symbols, ordering of beliefs and values, celebrations and rituals. While that story and tradition always held, in theory, the institution of service in sacred trust on behalf of the Church, this reality was often lost in the practical, committed enthusiasm of congregational members and in the stewardship and administrative policies of the religious congregation and the local Church.

The last thirty-five years (1970-2005) have occasioned for the Roman Catholic Church in the United States a new era of community, service, and witness. This new era returns us to the fundamental reality of the sacred trust and recognizes what those who founded religious congregations expressly reflected: institutions/programs/centers sponsored by religious congregations belong primarily to the Church and its mission. Regardless of the founding inspiration, what is essential and fundamental to these efforts in the name of the Church is the mission of the Church. That mission remains simply to continue the saving activity of Jesus Christ who came that "all might have life and have it more abundantly (John 10)." What is also important to these efforts is a careful reading of the historical and cultural processes within which and through which the Church and its mission are expressed:

> The People of God believes that it is led by the Spirit of the Lord who fills the whole world. Moved by that faith it tries to discern in the events, the needs, and the longings which it shares with other [persons]...what may be genuine signs of the presence or the purpose of God.[5]

Currently in the United States, religious congregations of women and men remain the largest group of sponsors of Catholic institutional services with the exception of elementary education and, perhaps, the institutional services of Catholic Charities. That situation is gradually shifting. The present and future vision regarding these institutional services, given our deepening understanding

[5] Vatican II, *Gaudium et spes*, 11, December 7, 1965: *AAS* 58(1966), 1030.

of "ministry as the commission and glory of all the baptized,"[6] suggests that the sustaining relationships of religious congregations will yield to partnerships among the faithful designed to maintain the vital gift of these institutional services within the mission of the Church. Parochial autonomy—whether diocesan or congregational—will yield to processes and commitments which obligate partners in service to transcend local, historically defined relationships.

Indeed, institutional venues for the works of mercy may be the first frontier for a reexamination of structures which have served the U.S. Church well in its first five hundred years, but may not serve its present or its future nearly so well. Current diocesan and parish structures and the semi-autonomous nature of the institutional ministry of religious congregations tend to fragment and duplicate essential services to persons in need. The complexity of human need and the interconnectedness of human experience suggest the necessity of global planning and system thinking even as implementation of service continues to be a local matter. The U.S. Catholic Church, along with many other national and international entities may need to learn new ways of organizing and new ways of relating. Institutions organized in the name of the Church's mission must be clear in their witness to Christian values, their commitment to be inclusive communities of service, their willingness to stand against personal and corporate patterns which impede life and occasion death, their openness to conservation of limited resources within natural and financial systems. How and by whom the U.S. Church will carry its energy of service into the next millennium remains a most pressing concern.

Documents such as *Ex Corde Ecclesiae*[7] and *A New Vision for a New Century* move in the right direction by recognizing institutional settings as vehicles of witness, proclamation, and service. However, effective structures and processes to adequately reflect that reality are either insufficient, inappropriate, or absent in many of the recommendations offered.

[6] Thomas O'Meara, *Theology of Ministry* (New York: Paulist Press, 1983), 3.

[7] John Paul II, apostolic constitution, *Ex corde Ecclesiae*, 15 August 1990, *AAS* 82(1990), 1475-1509.

A Case Study Approach to the Experience of Sponsorship

The last three decades of the twentieth century provide an excellent setting within which to explore the rich learning of religious congregations regarding the phenomenon of sponsorship. I will use primarily the experience of the Sisters of Mercy in the United States to describe the happenings in this arena, to name the learning, and to offer some reflections. I have chosen this methodology for two reasons: 1) this is the experience which is most familiar to me and from which I can speak with the greatest assurance; 2) the size and scope of this particular religious congregation is such that its trends and patterns often reflect a general paradigm as well as a particular one.

Three movements mark the experience and understanding of sponsorship in these closing decades of the twentieth century: activity around meaning and mission, activity around impact and influence, activity around preservation and collaboration. These movements are not mutually exclusive, nor are they necessarily sequential. In general, however, discussion and exploration of sponsorship tend to begin with attempts to articulate the meaning and mission embodied in institutional ministry, then to move to stabilize congregational influence and impact within this ministry, and, finally, to create processes and structures for preservation of congregational values and Catholic tradition and for collaboration with like-minded persons or organizations.

Meaning and Mission

The decade of the 1970s opened for religious congregations with a diligent and deliberate reexamination of their lives in community and service. The reexamination had been directed by the documents of Vatican II and the writings of Paul VI, especially *Perfectae caritatis*[8] and *Evangelica testificatio*[9]. The former encouraged up-to-date renewal of the life of religious congregations by a constant return to the sources of Christian life, the inspiration of the founder(s), and adaptation to the circumstances of the modern age. The latter exhorted religious congregations to treasure their call within the Church and to heed, in particular, the individual and collective cry of persons who are poor. The entire U.S. Church, of course, was involved in a similar reexamination.

[8] Vatican II, *Perfectae caritatis*, October 28, 1965: *AAS* 58(1966) 702-712.

[9] Paul VI, apostolic exhortation, *Evangelica testificatio*, June 29, 1971: *AAS* 63(1971) 757-787.

Jay Dolan, writing in *The American Catholic Experience*, described this decade as a "most turbulent period":

> Living in the midst of fundamental social and cultural changes and prodded by Vatican II to bring itself up to date, American Catholicism was about to pass through the most turbulent period of its short history. It was a time of both disillusionment and hope, of conflict and harmony, of crisis and growth.[10]

Religious congregations of women and men felt acutely this disillusionment and hope, conflict and harmony, and crisis. The effects on growth, however, were most dramatic. As sociologist Patricia Wittburg observes: "Whereas between 1950 and 1966, the number of religious in the U.S. rose over 23 percent, the subsequent two decades [saw] a decrease of over 30 percent."[11] This decrease converged with a renewed interest in the founding inspiration of each congregation, a call to be about the works of justice as well as mercy, and a flourishing of energy among other lay Catholics to active participation in the life of the Church. All these developments contributed to the creation of the new era of community, service, and witness mentioned earlier.

In this time of rediscovery of meaning and mission, the Sisters of Mercy of the Union and other religious congregations of women first addressed the question of sponsorship. An article written by Sr. Concilia Moran (October 1978) referred to a circular letter she had sent to the Sisters of Mercy of the Union in which she explicitly named the concern and the necessary exploration: [she identified sponsorship with] projects, programs, and institutions for which the Sisters...are corporately responsible." She went on in that same letter to define sponsorship as "support of, influence on and responsibility for a project, program or institution which furthers the goals of the sponsoring group.... Sponsorship...implies that the sponsoring group is publicly identified with the [entities], and makes certain resources available to them."[12]

As this letter indicates, religious congregations began to understand a responsibility not simply to this or that particular work of mercy (school, hospital, social service center), but to a system of works sustained by the members of the congregation over time and in many places. The possibilities of continuing to sustain these institutions into the future as well as the desirability of sustaining them alone became a constant topic of conversation at leadership

[10] Jay Dolan, *The American Catholic Experience* (New York: Image Books, 1985), 426.
[11] Patricia Wittberg, S.C., "Outward Orientation in Declining Organizations," in *Claiming Our Truth*, ed. Nadine Foley, O.P. (Washington, D.C.: Leadership Conference of Women Religious, 1988), 89.
[12] Letter is currently housed in the archives of the Institute of the Sisters of Mercy of the Americas, Silver Spring, Maryland.

gatherings, Chapter events, and task force meetings.[13] Coordination and centralization of strategic planning, personnel distribution, and financial allocation, consolidation, divestment and retrenchment, all began to be understood as necessary to stabilize the effective presence of members of the religious congregation in institutional ministries. While collaboration among and between members of religious congregations and their lay colleagues became a proactive and intentional choice for many congregations, the desired future envisioned by most was still a world in which a significant number of congregational members would share leadership and influence with other persons.

Several religious congregations of women and men organized their educational and health care institutions into networks, corporations, or associations. For example, in 1970, the Sisters of Mercy of the Union, Province of Detroit formed the Sisters of Mercy Health Corporation. The structure brought into one system the various health care institutions sponsored by the Sisters of Mercy, Province of Detroit. Collaboration in planning and key personnel decisions were largely internal as Board members and administrators were still mostly members of the religious congregation. However, a significant step toward collaboration with other lay Catholics was taken in the appointment of a layman as the corporation CEO and lay persons (Catholic and non-Catholic) to the Board of Trustees of the corporation.

In this same decade a Mercy Secondary Education Association was formed to provide a national forum to enhance and further the Mercy tradition in secondary education and a Mercy Higher Education Colloquium was formed with a similar purpose in higher education. Guided by a definition that suggested sponsorship was about relationship and impact, the Sisters of Mercy and others sought to strengthen congregational identity within their respective institutional ministry. They created forums to support individual members in their congregational identity as well as structures and processes that sought to invite lay colleagues to learn more about a specific tradition (e.g., Mercy, Dominican, Sacred Heart, Holy Names) and to join their energies in shaping institutional entities and endeavors.

[13] A General Chapter is the highest legislative body of a religious congregation. Delegates to a Chapter usually gather every four, five, or six years, depending on the specification of a particular congregation's governance document.

Congregational Influence and Impact

The struggle to articulate meaning and mission within a religious congregation's institutional ministry continued into the decade of the 1980s, but religious congregations of women and men also began to understand radical nuances to their service in the church that suggested new ways to be women and men religious as well as new ministries to reflect their specific story and tradition. An emphasis on the prophetic nature of religious life—that is, the witness to gospel values that the very life-form itself offered—and on the call to serve persons marginalized by poverty and discrimination moved many congregational members to new settings of community and service. Pastoral work, advocacy, and a variety of social services in non-institutional settings multiplied while institutional settings were often challenged and questioned as viable venues for carrying these new understandings. This movement to new venues coupled with a decline in new congregational members and the aging of existing members often occasioned a shortage of personnel to staff and maintain many institutional commitments.

The questioning of institutional works as viable venues for gospel witness and prophetic stance as well as the depletion of personnel to staff institutional works came at the very time that their growth and complexity necessitated business-oriented innovations and an emphasis on management skills and corporate policies that many congregational members found confusing and conflicting. Many Chapter sessions yielded passionate deliberations regarding whether to sponsor institutions of education and health care, how to sponsor such entities and with whom to sponsor. Many religious congregations determined to close, sell, merge, or transfer all or some of their institutional works. According to a study of sponsored works by the Leadership Conference of Women Religious, between 1985-1990 some two hundred institutions were involved in such activities, the largest numbers of those were institutions of secondary education or health care.[14]

Those congregations that determined to continue their sponsorship of institutions shifted from considerations of consolidation and coordination to strategic considerations of congregational influence and impact. For these congregations, the question was no longer "should we sponsor," but "how can we effectively sponsor with limited personnel and resources" and "how can we leverage sufficient control within collaboration to assure our meaning and mission?

[14] Anne Munley, IHM, *Threads for the Loom* (Washington, D.C.: Leadership Conference of Women Religious, 1992) 171.

Educational and formational programs for congregational members and lay colleagues became prominent as did value-driven criteria for continuing the congregation's relationship with any institutional work. The educational and formational programs strove to define and describe the responsibilities inherent in service in sponsored works of a particular congregation.

Collaboration among and between religious congregations grew in quality and in quantity. For example, the Sisters of Mercy of the Union, Province of Omaha established the Catholic Health Corporation in 1980. This Corporation, an early instance of co-sponsorship, united several distinct religious congregations in a deliberate effort to sustain the broadest base of purpose, i.e., the mission of the Church, while maintaining congregational identity and traditions at the local setting where service and relationships were happening.

This era of greater collaboration and cooperation among and between religious congregations surfaced also the possibility of tension between congregational impact and the broader impact of the local and/or universal church. Religious congregations had to learn to evaluate their own hopes for continued impact and relationship and the common good of the local church and/or persons in need of specific educational or health care services. For example, the Sisters of Mercy and other religious congregations attempted to organize and sustain their institutional ministry from a national perspective. In the instance of a Conference of Mercy Healthcare, local collaborations and identity eventually caused the demise of this effort intended to provide national identity and impact.

In education, this era of collaboration and cooperation remained largely a matter of networking within specific congregational works. The first Conference of Mercy Secondary Education (1981) brought together Sisters and lay colleagues from several countries to explore the meaning of Mercy secondary education in the twentieth century and to establish structures and processes to unify efforts to maintain a Mercy influence and impact in their various educational institutions. Presidents of Mercy institutes of higher education met annually during this decade of the 1980s with a similar purpose and hope. Congregational members who were faculty and staff of these same higher educational institutions also met to deepen understanding of the value and contribution of Mercy sponsored higher education and to name specific qualities and characteristics of the same.

Congregational leaders began to think strategically about institutional appointments and Board appointments: who might best further their sponsorship concerns? What positions within specific institutions and/or corporations might best insure congregational influence and impact? How to maintain effective identity within multiple venues of collaboration? What identity needs to be maintained (congregation's identity, Catholic identity, both/and)? Sponsorship programs and materials in education and health care multiplied. Gatherings of Boards of Trustees within and across health care and educational settings proliferated, as did position papers, vision statements, and evaluation tools to describe the expectations and perspectives of the sponsoring body, still largely congregations of women and men religious.

Preservation and Conservation

The new paradigm of community and service that had been evolving since the late 1960s became apparent in the last decade of the second millennium. Five elements in this new paradigm were affirmed in 1989 by a joint national gathering of leaders of religious congregations of women and men: prophetic witness, contemplative attitude toward life, poor and marginalized persons as the focus of ministry, spirituality of wholeness and global interconnectedness, and charism and mission as sources of identity.[15] This growing clarity regarding congregational identity and purpose serves as a partial explanation for changes discovered in the LCWR study quoted early. This valuable study scientifically verifies five trends in the service of members of religious congregations of women in the closing decade of the second millennium: movement from serving children and young adults to serving adults, movement from works owned or sponsored by the congregation to ministries not owned or sponsored by the congregation, movement from service with affluent or middle class communities to service with materially poor persons, movement from institutionally based services to non-institutionally based services, and movement from church related services to non-church related services.[16] Additional data verified other experiences within institutional ministry:

- projections indicated decreases by 1996 in the number of sponsored works in health care and elementary and secondary education, while increases were anticipated in housing, day care, free-standing clinics and hospices, and long-term care facilities

[15] At a joint Leadership Conference of Religious Women and Conference of Major Superiors of Men in Louisville, Kentucky in 1989, 1,100 women and men with leadership roles in their institutes generated ten *Transformative Elements* that they felt would characterize religious life by the year 2010. The five elements listed above received the highest affirmation in 1989.
[16] Munley, *Threads for the Loom*, 123.

- of the sponsored works sold in the previous five years (mid-1980s), 47 works continue to operate under other sponsorship (28 health care works, 8 high schools, 5 elementary schools, and 2 colleges)
- with the exception of secondary schools, at least 50 percent of respondents indicated that the ability of their institutes to continue their sponsored works was good or excellent.[17]

The study concluded that "the next three to five years are a crucial time for developing new sponsorship models and for building an infrastructure conducive to collaboration, mission effectiveness, and flexible response to emergent needs."[18]

For most congregations of women religious in the United States, then, the decade of the 1990s became a time to focus on preservation and conservation. The concerns of preservation centered on the deep story of the congregation and the fundamental Catholic identity of sponsored works. The concerns of conservation centered on allocation of scarce resources, deliberate selection of needy populations and marginalized peoples, simplification of systems, retention of relationships that were historical, geographical, and/or compatible in purpose and objectives.

The Eastern Mercy Health System expanded to form a co-sponsored health system, Catholic Health East. The new entity was formed through the coming together of twelve religious congregational sponsors[19] and their three health care systems. A similar movement occurred with the creation of Catholic Healthcare Partners and its several religious congregational sponsors and many health care institutions in Ohio, Kentucky, and Pennsylvania; and Catholic Health West and its several congregational sponsors and institutions in California and Arizona. The growing phenomenon of co-sponsorship brought into focus the radical importance of the preservation of Catholic health care. These co-sponsorship arrangements valued the preservation of a particular congregational tradition and spirit, but clearly saw this preservation as secondary to Catholic identity and the mission of the Church.

Educational institutions also began to move toward relationships that would secure a future for Catholic education in the United States as well as a future for educational institutions of specific religious congregations. Several networks of secondary education offered formative programs and organizational

[17] Ibid., 195-196.
[18] Ibid., 197.
[19] The Franciscan Sisters of Allegany, the Franciscan Sisters of St. Joseph, the nine regional communities of the Institute of the Sisters of Mercy, and the Sisters of Providence, Holyoke, MA.

support to the sponsored works of particular congregations, e.g., the Network of Sacred Heart Schools, Buttimer Institute of LaSallian Studies, Marist Leadership Institute.

Conversations among and between Mercy secondary and higher education leaders also began to highlight questions of preservation and conservation. In the case of sponsored educational institutions, however, the collaboration that seemed most desirable was based on the congregational tradition and spirit rather than historical and geographical realities. During the 1990s secondary educators and their religious sponsors formed a Network for Mercy Education to provide support and accountability for the integration of mission in Mercy secondary schools and to develop a unified structure that had the potential to hold full sponsorship responsibility for the Mercy community by about 2005. Similarly, a series of gatherings of sponsors and higher education presidents and administrators determined to create a Conference for Mercy Higher Education to coordinate and facilitate the ministry of Mercy higher education, to develop and recommend one or more models for sponsorship, and to support the identification and evaluation of Mercy-wide collaboration in programs and processes enhancing the mission in higher education.

Partnerships in a New Millennium

Partnership marks efforts within the area of sponsorship as a new millennium unfolds. The establishment of separate public juridic persons to maintain sponsoring relationships into the foreseeable future gains momentum in theoretical discussions and concrete decisions.[20] Programs of formation for leadership in these new realities are garnering considerable attention and resource. The Sisters of Mercy of the Americas currently participate in three new such entities: Catholic Health Ministries (a public juridic person sponsoring Trinity Health System), Hope Ministries (a public juridic person sponsoring Global Health Ministry, one component of Catholic Health East), and Catholic Health Care Federation (a public juridic person sponsoring those organizational members of Catholic Health Initiatives whose health care assets have been alienated by congregational sponsors). In the instance of Catholic Health Care

[20] Juridic persons are creations of [canon] law, [in the instance of the Church], that enable people to come together to perform a work they would be unable to do on their own. Public juridic persons operate in the name of the church; their temporal goods are ecclesiastical goods; they represent the church in the same sense that a diocese or religious congregation does. (Francis Morrisey, OMI, "Toward Juridic Personality" in *Sponsorship: Current Challenges and Future Directions* (reprinted from *Health Progress*, Catholic Health Association, July-August 2001), 10.

Federation the religious congregation has transferred already a significant portion of ministerial patrimony to the new public juridic person. The generosity of givers and recipients marks this transaction as an historical moment within the Sisters of Mercy and within the Church in the United States.

Mercy secondary and higher education institutions do not envision such dramatic gestures of conservation and partnership in the near future. However, the new sponsorship models developed in the Network of Mercy Education (secondary and elementary institutions) and in the Conference of Mercy Higher Education call for significant involvement of lay colleagues at the highest levels of decision-making and significant plans for formation of all leadership persons within these ministries.

Sponsorship Academies, formation programs and mission driven criteria for Board membership, CEO selection, and evaluation of programs and budgets in both health care and education continue to be refined and improved to assure attention to the deeper story of these ministerial settings, the living story of their Catholic and Mercy identity.

Epilogue

Congregational leaders stand in the midst of a number of groupings defined first by their leadership role in their religious institute. Their primary purpose as congregational leaders is the preservation of the charism and tradition of the congregation, the common good of the congregation and its membership, and the authenticity of the apostolic works as expressions of the mission of the Church and the particular nuance of the congregation's heritage. Congregational leaders serve the whole Church best when they act out of this rich context of service and witness. Bearing a story or a tradition never obligates us to replicate the past, but rather, with its legacy, to be responsible participants in the present moment. Responsible participation suggests an active engagement of circumstances with imaginative freedom to move those circumstances toward the fullness of human experience, toward the kingdom of our God.

CHAPTER TWO

Various Types of Sponsorship

FRANCIS G. MORRISEY, OMI

Introduction

When we speak of sponsorship and its implications, we can look at it from many perspectives: the underlying theology, the canonical structures, the forms of functioning, the various models, and so forth. Not surprisingly, in this paper, it is our intention to look at its implications from the perspective of canon law.

Yet, like so many other things in the world, this perspective is not something static. Canon law is changing rapidly. Already, the "new" Code promulgated in 1983 is obsolete, or at least seriously dated, in many aspects. When it was promulgated, for instance, the Iron Curtain was still in place, the Internet and its implications for communication and knowledge proliferation did not exist, the sexual abuse scandal had not reared its ugly head and the law was not designed to address the issue when it arose, religious institutes had not begun pooling their resources, public juridic persons for health care were not a known commodity in the Church, and so forth. After promulgation of the Code, norms governing Catholic colleges and universities were issued in *Ex corde Ecclesiae* in 1990.[1] In 2005, the Instruction *Dignitas connubii* reworked considerably the norms on matrimonial nullity processes, taking into account developments in jurisprudence and practice since 1983.[2]

[1]. See John Paul II, apostolic constitution, "*Ex corde Ecclesiae*", August 15, 1990, *AAS*, 82(1990) 1475-1509.

[2]. See Pontifical Council for the Interpretation of Legislative Texts, instruction, *Dignitas connubii*, January 25, 2005, Libreria editrice vaticana, 2005, 223p.

So, canon law – like its counterparts in the secular world – evolves to respond to new needs. It is not the role of law to be creative, or to force new structures or principles on people; rather, it takes the common wisdom and tries to express it in terms that allow for future development.

Structures are usually tailor-made; one size does not fit all. Therefore, there are a variety of them available in canon law to support apostolic activities. Among such structures, we find various kinds of associations of the faithful (*de facto*, private, public); juridic persons (diocesan or pontifical, public or private); other entities that do not have a formal canonical status, although they enjoy various forms of tacit recognition;[3] and entities that function under a civil title and group various canonical entities together.[4] The determination of which structure is the most appropriate will depend on local circumstances and needs.

Furthermore, since circumstances are changing rapidly, what was considered to be an appropriate – or even an ideal – form of structure at a given moment, could soon find itself left behind as circumstances change. Therefore, one principle to be kept in mind whenever re-structuring of sponsorship takes place, is to allow for future development and adjustments. Whatever is proposed and adopted ought not be not inscribed in stone as it may well have to be adjusted or even changed in subsequent years.

When, following the Vatican II insights, the restructuring of Church educational and healthcare institutions began to take place in the late 1960s and 1970s, the focus was on ownership of property. However, in recent years, there has been a clear movement away from this ownership model since, in many situations, ownership is not clear, and there are contradictions between the civil understanding of the term and its canonical usage. Indeed, when dealing with not-for-profit undertakings, we do not speak of "ownership", but of "members" who are responsible for the undertaking. To help us understand the evolution of sponsorship models, it would be good to set a base. We would then be in a position to see how forms of sponsorship have evolved. Following that, we could look at variations and consider briefly where such trends could lead us in the years ahead.

3. Among such entities, there are associations which are civilly recognized, but which do not have formal canonical recognition, such as the various Canon Law Societies existing in many parts of the world.

4. Among these, there are a number of healthcare systems that do not, as a system, have formal canonical status, but which carry out their church responsibilities through the various public juridic persons which have come together to establish the system.

Understanding the Background of Sponsorship

Terms Being Used

What is sponsorship?

The term sponsorship is not found in the *Code of Canon Law*. It is generally accepted, though, that within the Church *sponsorship* entails three important elements: (1) the use of one's name; (2) the exercise of certain governance responsibilities that arise from this use; and (3) some form of accountability to Church authorities. Not surprisingly, then, this entails elements of "quality control". Traditionally, *sponsorship* referred more to a position of corporate strength and independence through ownership and some form of control via reserved powers. Today, however, as new relations are established with other providers, the involvement of sponsors relies more on their ability to influence than to control. Hand in hand with this evolution, questions of ownership are becoming more and more blurred and even less important.

Even in day-to-day parlance, without reference to the Church, the term *sponsorship* has a number of meanings. A sponsor can be someone who supports or pays for a specific program, or who stands in for another. In France, the term "*tutelle*" is used frequently, and, in English, it could mean either "guardianship" or "administrative supervision". In Quebec, the most common expression is "*la relève institutionnelle*", which means to "take over from someone", indicating a change in responsibility.

For our purposes, we could use a practical definition that is subject to change with time: Sponsorship of an apostolate or ministry is a formal relationship between a recognized Catholic organization and a legally formed entity entered into for the sake of promoting and sustaining the Church's mission in the world.[5]

A few words of explanation would help:

- when the definition speaks of an "apostolate or ministry", it indicates a corporate work, as distinguished from the work of individuals;

[5]. The reader will note many similarities with the definition proposed, in a healthcare context, by The Catholic Health Association of the USA in its 2005 working paper, "Towards a Theology of Catholic Health Care Sponsorship – A Work in Progress," pg. 9.

- a "formal relationship" would presuppose one that is guaranteed both by canon law and by civil law;
- the term "recognized" is used to indicate approval either by the diocesan bishop or by the Holy See;
- the word "organization" refers to a religious institute, a group of institutes acting as co-sponsors, a diocese, a public juridic person, or any other canonical entity (such as an association of the faithful). While the canonical juridical person is itself the sponsor, it functions through specific individuals designated to carry out the duties of sponsorship;
- the expression, "the Church's mission in the world" was designed to cover the various activities carried out by the Catholic Church in furtherance of the mission entrusted to it by its founder.
- It follows that the definition used here could apply to Catholic Charities, to educational institutions, to works of social service, and to healthcare institutions.

Ownership

"Ownership" is another term that is not directly found in the *Code of Canon Law*, although it too is commonly used. The code prefers to use the Latin *dominium*, a word that implies limited rights, as distinct from the full rights which we often associate with full ownership (such as the right to use and to *abuse* property). According to Catholic theology and canonical practice, temporal goods of the Church are not "owned" by individuals, but are entrusted to their care for a specific mission. Goods belonging to the Church cannot be distributed to family members, nor are they part of the administrator's estate upon death.

It would be good to keep in mind that when we use the term ownership among ourselves, we are really using it in this restricted or limited sense. In the past, the concepts of ownership and sponsorship were generally interrelated. It was commonly held, for instance, that, for a work to be sponsored, the sponsoring institute had to hold title to it and exercise control over it. However, such an opinion is not held today because there are so many instances where institutes sponsor institutions without having any direct ownership rights over them.

A point to keep in mind when dealing with the civil counterpart of this notion, and which was alluded to earlier, is that there are no owners when we are dealing with a not-for-profit corporation. Thus, a separately incorporated educational institution, even though sponsored by a Catholic juridic person, is not considered civilly to be owned by the Church. There are members who are involved on behalf of the corporation. This distinction led to a number of misunderstandings in educational institutions, as the so-called McGrath thesis[6] was followed by many Catholic universities and colleges, and the Church was considered no longer to have any say over the property and assets.[7]

Sponsorship and Governance

As we shall see shortly when we study the evolution of forms of sponsorship, and in view of the stronger emphasis now being placed on mission, the way in which governance responsibilities and sponsorship duties have evolved in recent years, shows clearly, as was the case with ownership, that although the two are closely related, they are quite different.

Governance usually entails some type of role in establishing policy. It is more concerned with the actual functioning or running of an undertaking, and establishes clear lines of internal accountability within the work for decisions taken and activities conducted. For this, governance is considered to be internal to the activity.

On the other hand, sponsorship will refer more directly now to relationships and to the spirit in which an undertaking is carried out. The sponsors will be more particularly focused on the mission and its quality, rather than on its actual delivery. Sponsorship also has a relation to the "outside", in the sense that it is through sponsorship that, in the case of a Catholic undertaking, it will be accountable to church authorities.

There is no incompatibility between the two. If qualified persons are readily available, they can obviously assume both sets of responsibilities, as was the case for years. But, today, the distinctions between the two are becoming clearer, even though the same persons might be involved in both. In recent years, as situations evolved, and as the delivery of health care (to use that example)

6. See John J. McGrath, *Catholic Institutions in the United States: Canonical and Civil Law Status* (Washington, DC: The Catholic University of America Press, 1968) McGrath's thesis held that at the moment of civil incorporation the institution's goods ceased to be ecclesiastical goods.

7. See also, Congregation for Catholic Education, January 2, 1974 and October 7, 1974, in *Canon Law Digest*, 9, 367-371: "...We have not been unaware of the growing tendency for the ecclesiastical entities that own and operate these institutions [i.e., Catholic colleges and universities in the USA] to alienate them from ecclesiastical control and ownership, frequently through civil corporate structural changes (Boards of Trustees, Regents, etc.), often citing the 'McGrath thesis' as justification for this action, an action that takes place without ecclesiastical approbation. ...Each Bishop and Major Superior responsible in any way for an institution of higher learning is to send us appropriate information on how the Catholic character of the institution is being maintained and about the exact civil and canonical status of the institution." It was after this document was issued that owners began speaking about "Catholic identity" of their institutions.

became more sophisticated and even somewhat complicated because of government regulations, new medical techniques, and the complexity of operations, it was found to be more beneficial for church undertakings to place their limited resources of time and persons on the sponsorship level, leaving the governance responsibilities to those who were more directly qualified for this particular type of work. In educational institutions, the problem was not felt in the same acute way since many congregational leadership roles were filled by persons who had previously been involved in this ministry.

Ministry and Mission

Sponsorship has little if any meaning if it is not related more particularly to the mission and ministry of the Church. The Church's mission is threefold: to teach, to sanctify, and to serve through governance. In a Catholic context, sponsors must be able to articulate what they consider to be the non-negotiables for the Catholic ministry, yet be flexible enough to choose between total control at one end of the spectrum and, at the other, having some presence, with the potential to influence. The process demands a commitment to collaboration with others in order to make a smooth transition to new forms of service delivery.

For this reason, present-day sponsors have to consider which structures or processes would best maintain Catholic control or influence. How can they really influence and guide the works carried out in their name? Possible approaches include sponsorship covenants, careful selection of leadership, some type of board majority, establishment of appropriate mediation and arbitration processes, and so forth. There is no one answer to this question; much depends on a complex of factors driving the mission and the apostolic works.

The Evolution of Sponsorship Arrangements[7]

In order to understand how sponsorship arrangements have evolved, a number of steps in the recent evolution of sponsorship roles can be traced, although not every institution went through all these steps or did so in the same order. Because it was in the area of healthcare that the evolution was most evident, this example will illustrate the evolution. Although not as evident, there were some similar types of movement in the field of Catholic education, especially for the first few models to be listed below.

The Early Model – Religious Sponsorship

The most common form of sponsorship in the past derived from direct dominium over the property and the active presence and involvement in operations of many persons identified with the sponsor (for instance, religious on staff). The name of the sponsoring institute was often found in the name of the institution and its members were directly involved in the delivery of the service.

Lay Advisory Boards

After the Vatican II period, more emphasis began to be placed in church circles on the dignity of the baptismal vocation, moving away from an almost exclusive reliance on the vocations of priesthood and religious consecration. For this reason, more and more lay persons became directly involved in the decision-making processes and in leadership positions. Sometimes, in educational institutions, this was through boards of trustees, or regents; in healthcare, advisory boards were often established. At the same time, the number of available religious began to diminish.

Lay-religious Governing Boards

With time, and also because of these factors, the duties of sponsorship became more identified with those of a board of directors and the establishment of policy, rather than with the actual delivery of services.

At various stages in the process, certain works acquired a civil recognition (i.e., civil incorporation or something similar, depending on the country) distinct from that of the sponsoring religious institute. This led to the establishment of boards of directors whose membership sometimes coincided with that of the sponsoring institute's corporate board.

Then, there came about a further separation as a two-tiered structure was put in place: a distinction was made between the members of the corporation, and the board of directors. Division of authority between the members and the board was directed by the use of "reserved powers". It was at this point in the development that Catholic institutions of higher learning went through a process that was slightly different from that followed by healthcare institutions, since many of the former, when restructuring, did not advert in their corporate documents to the notion of reserved powers. Indeed, the situation continues today, although church authorities do not recognize that alienation of property took place when the structures were changed, or, if alienation did take place , that it was not valid canonically (canon 1296).[8]

The Code of Canon Law makes little reference to what are now known as reserved powers. When they were first being considered as an acceptable way to establish clear lines of authority, there could have been as many as fourteen or so reserved powers that institutes considered to be essential, because they did not wish to relinquish control over their institutions too easily. The well-known work by Adam Maida and Nicholas Cafardi, *Church Property, Church Finances, and Church-related Corporations*, addressed this issue in detail in 1984.[9] Among the original reserved powers, in addition to the ones generally still in place today, were also found: approval of the operating budgets, the ratification of appointments to various offices (not just the appointment of the CEO and of board members), approval of the auditor, etc.

With time, the number of what were considered to be essential reserved powers was shortened, as sponsors become more comfortable with the idea of having others directly involved; these newer essential powers now focused on three particular areas: on documents (corporate documents and by-laws), on persons (CEO and Board) and on property (alienation of land and buildings, mortgages, bond issues).

Then, to facilitate coordination and to reduce expenses, systems began to be established, grouping several institutions, usually sponsored by the same religious institute. This resulted in a further refinement of reserved powers, with some being operative at an intermediate level (that of the system), rather than at the level of membership.

[8] Many of the ideas in this section are expressed in my study, "Catholic Identity in a Challenging Environment", in *Health Progress*, 80, No. 6 (1999) 38-42.

[9]. See (then) Archbishop J. Rigali, "St. Louis University Hospital Sold to For-Profit Corporation", February 24, 1998, in *Origins*, 27(1997-1998), pp. 629, 631-633):"The important issues regarding the applicability of canon law to St. Louis University which came to the surface in connection with the sale of St. Louis University hospital have been authoritatively addressed by the Holy See at the highest level of the Church. Although the authorization granted by the Holy See for the sale of the hospital was not delayed until the governance structure of St. Louis University would have a mechanism whereby the Society of Jesus can exercise its own proper measure of control with respect to the University to ensure its compliance with canon law, the Holy See considers this mechanism to be a matter of great importance to avoid conflict in the future."

Inter-congregational Sponsorship

More recently, a number of institutes have come together to sponsor their works jointly and to operate inter-congregational systems. When they did so, the reserved powers were originally exercised separately for institutions owned by a particular institute, as distinct from those owned by another sponsor. However, with time this became overly complicated as funds and operations became more and more mingled.

Not surprisingly, then, a further step occurred soon afterwards, when many of these powers were delegated jointly on a permanent basis to the new board to represent the joint sponsors, with only the property ownership issues or similar matters being reserved to the original sponsors.

Today, canonists are refining their thinking about what is required in relation to property ownership and stable patrimony. While, previously, buildings as such were almost automatically considered to be stable patrimony, today, with depreciation, it can happen that a certain building has little if any book value, and at times even risks becoming a major liability because of the state of the building (for instance, presence of asbestos) or of the limitations imposed by insurance payment plans, capitation, etc. Also, closer investigation shows that many of the funds identified with an institution are not congregational funds as such, but rather are goods held in trust and administered by the sponsors. This has led to a number of important canonical distinctions, particularly as regards the preparation of detailed inventories (see canon 1283) which take into account the various ways in which the assets were acquired. Intentions of donors are primordial in helping to resolve certain dilemmas. The question is often asked, for instance, whether the goods were given to the institution itself (for instance, to fund a new library) or to the sponsoring religious institute.

One of the advantages underlying this new form of cooperation – which moves away from ownership issues – lies in the fact that the Catholic character and the mission of the work take on more importance than the particular charism of the original sponsoring institute. Indeed, at times, it was difficult to determine what were the component elements of a particular charism. Institutes are now coming together to further as one the mission of Christ.

Moving to New Forms of Lay-Religious-Diocesan Sponsorship

It was not uncommon for an institute and a diocese to come together to operate certain institutions and works jointly (as, for instance, certain consolidated high schools and institutions of higher learning, or nursing homes owned by the diocese and operated by the healthcare system sponsored by the religious institute). In such instances, it became appropriate to establish new diocesan church corporations, known as juridic persons, to assume canonical sponsorship of the joint works. The works then took on a life of their own, distinct from that of the original sponsoring institute or diocese. This approach is just now beginning to be used for Catholic institutions of higher learning, particularly in the case of consolidated schools.

Where healthcare systems were established, they often overlapped diocesan boundaries, and were sometimes co-sponsored; it thus became appropriate or even necessary to have a higher authority grant distinct canonical recognition to the system, so that it would become self-sponsored. There do not seem to be too many similar systems in the field of education.[10] The need to obviate difficulties of jurisdiction explains the more recent involvement of the Holy See in granting new types of recognition (either public juridic personality, or private juridic personality,[11] depending on the situation) to works carried out in common by a number of sponsors.

Various models of public juridic persons have been approved, either by diocesan Bishops[12] or by the Holy See. Among those approved by the Holy See, in some instances, the entire system has been granted juridic personality (as is the case with Covenant Health Systems in Lexington, MA).[13] In others, a component part was granted such a canonical status (as with Hope Ministries within Catholic Health East).[14] In some instances, all the members are Catholics; in others (such as Trinity Health) a majority of the members must be Catholics.[15] In some, the bishops are among the members;[16] in others, it is almost solely lay persons who comprise the membership.

10. See A. MAIDA and N. CAFARDI, *Church Property, Church Finances, and Church-related Corporations*, St. Louis, CHA of the United States, 1984, xxii-339p., at pp. 155-163. (Reprinted 2000: Pittsburgh, Duquesne University School of Law).

11. Perhaps the Conference of Mercy Higher Education, based in Chicago, would be the best example of such a "system" in the educational field, although it does not enjoy distinct canonical status at the time of writing.

12. An example of private juridic personality can be found in PeaceHealth, approved by the Holy See on April 29, 1997.

13. An example of a diocesan public juridic person for health care is Providence Health Care, established in the Archdiocese of Vancouver, Canada, June 22, 1999, replacing a previous diocesan juridic person known as "CHARA", and established on October 7, 1994.

14. The canonical statutes of Covenant Health Systems were approved by decree of the Holy See, July 18, 1995.

15. The canonical statutes of Hope Ministries were approved by decree of the Holy See, July 7, 2000.

16. The canonical statutes of Catholic Health Ministries were approved by decree of the Holy See, July 14, 2000.

Other Forms of Collaboration

Before too long, there were calls for joint ventures or partnership with other-than-Catholic providers, whether they were faith-based or purely secular. This led to the need of determining clearly what were the conditions according to which Catholic sponsors could indeed partner with others. This development has caused a certain amount of unease in various circles. In the area of healthcare, it became compounded when certain civil governments ordered that all healthcare providers within a given geographical area be united under regional boards or the equivalent. In educational works, there could be complications when there is a consortium of colleges or universities where students can take credited courses at various establishments, even though not all the institutions that are partnered together are subject to the provisions of *Ex corde Ecclesiae*.

Another development which has not been well received in many circles, but which cannot simply be dismissed, is that Catholic sponsors or providers were asked on occasion to partner with investor-owned facilities. This involvement with the for profit corporations puts into question the Church's long-standing tradition of offering services, not for personal benefit, but for the upbuilding of society and the Church community.

In addition there are now a number of efforts on the part of certain religious institutes to have all their apostolic works – whether in education, or in social services, or in healthcare – grouped together under a single juridic person, distinct from the institute itself. To date such projects have not yet come to fruition in actuality, but they are being seriously considered, particularly in Australia.[17]

VARIATIONS ON THE THEME OF SPONSORSHIP

Various Types of Sponsors and Related Issues

As we have seen from this overview, there are many ways of sponsoring church-related works. One is not better than the other; nor does the adoption of one model signify that no others may be considered in the years ahead.

Generally speaking, in the Church there are four recognized categories of sponsors: (1) institutes of consecrated life and societies of apostolic life; (2)

17. The recent undertakings of the St. John of God Sisters (healthcare), and the Sisters of Charity in Australia (healthcare, education, social services) are indicative of this search for new sponsorship structures.

dioceses; (3) public juridic persons; (4) associations of the faithful. While, in some instances, each category of sponsor acts separately, in others, especially where systems have been established, we find overlapping forms of sponsorship, where dioceses and institutes co-sponsor certain works together.

Different models have been chosen. One interesting model is found in Catholic Health Sponsors of Ontario, as noted above, a pontifical public juridic person established by the Holy See in 1997.[18] The members are representatives of the original sponsoring religious congregations, as well as representatives of the Catholic Health Association of Ontario (bishops and sponsors). Provision is made that, if an original sponsor wishes to withdraw from this form of ministry, the seats on the membership board will be assumed by the Catholic Health Association. In this way, continuity is assured, and a close relationship with the bishops of Ontario is guaranteed. This might not be feasible in certain areas, but it works well in Ontario.

Civilly Established Sponsorship

In addition to the various canonical models, there are other civil or legislated models in place which do not rely directly and immediately on Catholic identity. Rather, their ecclesial mission comes from the identity of the parties that make up the system, although the system itself does not have canonical personality. Many of these are listed in the *Official Catholic Directory*, thus indicating that Catholic identity has been recognized by the diocese in which they are located. Ascension Health is a good example of this approach. It is the largest Catholic healthcare system in the USA at the present time, deriving its sponsorship not from the structure of the system, but from the identity of the sponsors who comprise it. Ascension Health does not have formal canonical recognition as a system. The same could be said of Catholic Health East. Likewise for a number of educational institutions which formerly had a direct relationship with a diocese or an institute, but which have since established new forms of relationships. St. Edward's University in Austin, TX, is an example of such. It is recognized as Catholic, but is no longer directly and formally sponsored by the Congregation of the Holy Cross.

In other words, Catholic "identity" is not necessarily reduced to canonical structures. A bishop can decide to grant recognition to a group that is recognized

18. For instance, the statutes of "Catholic Health Sponsors of Ontario" were approved by decree of the Holy See, November 24, 1997. The canonical documents provide that if an original sponsor wishes to withdraw, the sponsor's seat will be assumed by an appointee of the Catholic Health Association of Ontario, composed of the Bishops of Ontario and the other sponsors (By-laws, Art. 2.2).

civilly as having a Catholic purpose, and which furthers the mission of the church, without having any particular canonical structure to back it up. This may not be an ideal situation, but it would be important to keep in mind the distinction between Catholic identity and Catholic sponsorship. Probably Catholic Charities as they exist in certain dioceses,[19] or the St. Vincent de Paul Society would be good examples of this approach. There is nothing more "Catholic" than either of these, yet they do not have formal canonical establishment or status (at least in most instances). Another instance comes to mind: a group of lay persons could wish to open a home for the elderly and would like to have it recognized as Catholic; they even provide a chapel on the premises. The diocesan bishop could agree to recognize the work as Catholic, even though it has not been canonically established and is not part of the diocesan properties or works. As such, there is no canonical sponsor, yet the work has Catholic identity.

Some Possible Future Trends

At this point, I would like to offer some personal considerations. These are not, as such, based in canon law, but they seem to derive from the life and mission of the church, at least in North America.

Fortunately, a new era in collaboration is seeing the light of day in the church. Things are happening today with institutes and dioceses working together, that would have been unthinkable thirty years ago. We do not want to lose this impetus. Nevertheless, in spite of the pooling of resources, there is a real danger that we will lose our Catholic institutions from within, since on so many occasions, in spite of legal structures in place, there appears to be lacking a will or a desire to carry out a mission in harmony with Church teachings. Or, if there is the desire to do so, do we have the competent persons available who can make "catholicity" a continuing reality?

This will call for extensive dialogue with all Church representatives, not only within the country (bishops, conference of bishops, etc), but also at the level of the Holy See.

Sponsorship today is not something focused on ownership and property issues. Rather, the focus must be on the mission. Yet, more and more, those

19. In many instances, however, "Catholic Charities" are a direct work of the diocese, even though they have distinct corporate existence.

involved are becoming distanced from the actual mission which is carried out by others. Their involvement is more at the policy level.

It seems that, today, Church leaders should be more concerned with the formation of board members and with their preparation for sponsorship responsibilities.

Since sponsorship as a term is becoming less and less clear when we look at its applications from the perspective of a few years ago, the vocabulary used might have to be adjusted along the way. The term sponsorship is not threatening, but does it really convey what is involved today?

CONCLUSION

The points presented here are not absolute statements. The issues and challenges raised in the church today will probably not be the ones our successors will have to face ten years from now. As we look back on the evolution of our sponsorship models, we can see how a gradual but steady shift in focus came to the fore. The process is not over.

We can no longer keep on operating under past models. They simply are not adequate to today's world. However, we have not yet found the answer to the model that will resolve all our difficulties. We probably never will find such an answer.

If we believe in the Church's mission, and if we believe firmly in the "Catholic" dimension of such apostolic activities, then there is no reason to stop our efforts. But, if we do not, then let's get out of it before we ruin what others have done before us!

We don't have all the answers; we probably don't even have all the questions yet. But, at least, let us keep on trying!

CHAPTER THREE

From the Heart of the Church to the Heart of the World: Ownership, Control and Catholic Identity of Institutional Apostolates in the United States

JOHN P. BEAL

Introduction

Jesus sent out his disciples "ahead of him in pairs to every town and place he intended to visit" to cure the seek and announce the nearness of God's reign. With "no money bag, no sack, no sandals," this first contingent of disciples was singularly unprepared for the challenges that faced them; nonetheless, their mission was surprisingly successful.[1] Subsequent generations of disciples have also accepted Jesus' call to bring the good news to the towns and places to which they were sent or in which they found themselves. Often as ill-prepared and under-resourced as the first band, these subsequent generations of disciples went forth, sometimes one by one, sometimes two by two, but more often as communities and associations, to respond to the multiple material and spiritual needs of the people they encountered on the way. If the French Modernist Alfred Loisy could say with more admiration than irony that "Jesus proclaimed the Kingdom of God, but what came was the Church,"[2] a contemporary historian might say that Jesus' disciples proclaimed the Kingdom of God, but what developed were institutional apostolates.

[1] See Luke 10:1-20.

[2] Alfred Loisy, *L'Évangile et l'Église* (Paris: A. Picard et Fils, 1902) 111.

The achievement of many generations of disciples in North America is evident today in the array of institutional apostolates, some still thriving and some now struggling, in the fields of education and health care, charity and social service, which continue to dot our landscape. These apostolic institutions were born from the hearts of countless individuals and groups, religious institutes and dioceses, but, in their deepest sense, they were "born from the heart of the Church,"[3] i.e., out of the heart of "the whole vast body of people that once arose out of the event of Christ and lives still to bring him to the world for its redemption."[4] In this Church, identity and mission are inextricably intertwined.

> The church is the people distinguished from all other human communities by a faith, hope, and love that derive from and center around Jesus Christ. Its mission derives immediately from this identity, for even by its very existence the church, as the social and historical sign of Christ's redemptive work, exists in order, as its instrument, to keep alive the memory of Jesus of Nazareth, to communicate his offer of salvation, and to reflect his light and to offer his power for the shaping of human history, both individual and collective.[5]

Identity and mission must be similarly intertwined in apostolic institutions if they are to remain in the Church out of whose heart they were born.

THE SEAMLESS GARMENT BEGINS TO UNRAVEL: 1960–2005

Institutional Apostolates in 1960

At their origins and for most of their history, the inherence of these apostolic institutions in the communion of the Church was as unproblematic as it was unquestioned. For the most part, they were founded and built, owned and operated, governed and inspired by the religious institutes, and more rarely dioceses, which had conceived them and brought them to birth. The influence of the sponsoring religious body in these institutional apostolates was pervasive. The evangelical charisms of the founders were embodied not only in the cold prose of corporate charters but also in the warm presence of members of

[3] John Paul II, apostolic constitution *Ex corde Ecclesiae*, August 15, 1990, §1: *AAS* 82 (1990) 1475.
[4] Joseph Komanchak, "The Catholic University in the Church," in *Catholic Universities in Church and Society*, ed. John P. Langan (Washington, DC: Georgetown University Press, 1993) 38.
[5] Ibid., 35-36.

the sponsoring bodies from the board rooms to the laundry rooms of health care facilities and from the classrooms to the athletic fields and residence halls of educational institutions. So intimate was the relationship between sponsoring Church body and its institutional apostolates that their internal Catholic substance and their external links to the larger Catholic community were woven together in what seemed like a seamless garment. While it is important that this earlier era not be viewed nostalgically as a lost golden age, it was an era in which questions about the ecclesial or, more particularly, the Catholic identity and mission of institutional apostolates could be–and largely were–assumed rather than subjected to agonized questioning and endless strategizing. However, that era in the history of institutional apostolates is over; the seamless garment has begun to unravel.

Factors Contributing to the Unraveling

The easy and almost instinctive identification of ownership, sponsorship and ecclesial identity of institutional apostolates became increasingly problematic in the wake of the Second Vatican Council and the ecclesiological upheavals it occasioned. The Council's shift from an ecclesiological paradigm that emphasized the Church's juridic dimension to one that was couched in the language of communion, its abandonment of a fortress mentality in the face of the modern world in favor of a warm embrace of it, its call for religious institutes to renew themselves by recovering and reinvigorating their founding charisms, and its openness to a role for lay people, and even non-Catholics, in the life and mission of the Church, all had practical implications for the institutional expressions of the Church's work of education and charity. While the impact of post-conciliar movements of reform and renewal in the Church in general and in their sponsoring religious institutes on apostolic institutions cannot be gainsaid, institutional apostolates were also affected deeply by other trends in North American society, which have not always received due attention, especially in canonical literature. I will cite only four of these:

1. The changing complexion of the American Catholic population: American Catholics have always been the traditional target or clientele for institutional apostolates. However, by 1960, the composition of the Catholic population of the United States had changed markedly from the poor, huddled masses who had come as waves of immigrants in the nineteenth and early twentieth centuries. No longer were American Catholics primarily uneducated immigrants living in the tenements of

central cities; they had increasingly become reasonably well educated, native-born, middle class suburbanites. The movement of Catholics into the middle (and now upper) class, out of the center cities into suburbia, toward ever greater educational and professional attainments, and into increasing affluence has continued unabated.[6] (Before consigning "immigrant Catholicism" to the dustbins of history, however, it is worth recalling that most of the recent growth and most of the projected future growth of the Catholic population of the United States has been and will be among relatively poor and poorly educated immigrants, especially Hispanics.) This "gentrification" of the native-born Catholic population has made them more discriminating consumers of the services provided by Catholic apostolic institutions. At the very least, it has forced apostolic institutions to market themselves as much for their excellence as for their Catholicity.

2. Increasing complexification, specialization, and professionalization: Especially in health care and education but also in other areas in which apostolic activities are conducted, fields have become increasingly specialized and those who provide services in them increasingly professionalized. General practitioners have been supplanted by specialists, and not only professional courtesy but professional ethics bar practitioners from crossing the boundaries of their specialties. As a result, it is much more difficult than it once was to move effortlessly from a successful tenure in the operating room to a successful term in the board room or to shift from classroom teaching to educational administration. Rapid advances in knowledge in general and science and technology in particular have made the provision of health care and education vastly more complex than anything the founding mothers and fathers of apostolic institutions could have envisaged. In health care, the simple dispensary has been replaced by the high tech hospital; in education, concern for computer literacy has overtaken concern for inculcating the "three R's." Complexification has, in turn, accelerated the pace of specialization and professionalization in the medical and educational fields. As a result, it has become increasingly difficult for religious sponsors of institutional apostolates to know what is really

[6] See James Davidson, et al., *The Search for Common Ground: What Unites and Divides Catholic Americans* (Huntington, IN: Our Sunday Visitor, 1997); Andrew Greeley, *The American Catholic: A Social Portrait* (New York: Basic Books, 1977); and George Gallup and Jim Castelli, *The American Catholic People: Their Beliefs, Practices and Values* (New York: Doubleday, 1987).

happening in their institutions, much less what are the implications of this activity for the religious character of the institution.

3. The decreasing number of religious and priests serving in these apostolates: The declining numbers of active religious and priests in the United States has entailed their shrinking presence in Catholic institutional apostolates. Those who remain associated with the institutions are either increasingly disengaged from their day-to-day life or relegated, and perhaps marginalized, to specialized areas dealing with "religious stuff." With the decline of the "ministry of presence," positions in institutions formerly held by members of the sponsoring institution have increasingly been taken by lay people, who usually lack the extended formation in the charism of the sponsoring institute and grounding in the traditions of the apostolic institution that priests and religious enjoyed. The growing complexity of modern institutions and specialization of fields encourages employees of institutional apostolates to see their work simply as jobs and not as participation in a ministry. As a result, providing formation in charism and ministry to the next generation of largely lay leaders and participants in the institutional apostolate has become a critical challenge for those who would retain some discernible ecclesial identity for these institutions.

4. The commodification of health care and education: In the United States, medical care and education have increasingly become services to be bought and sold like any other commodity on the market.[7] Health care and educational institutions, the purveyors of these services, are subject to the same market forces as other business enterprises. They must compete with other providers of the same service for market share and, thus, must market themselves aggressively if they are to attract enough paying customers to survive and prosper in this intensely competitive environment. Treating health care, education and other services traditionally provided by church-related agencies as commodities fits awkwardly in a tradition that has viewed these services as forms of Christian compassion and their provision as a ministry. Not surprisingly, this market orientation has sometimes openly clashed with the evangelical impetus of institutional apostolates but has more often been subtly corrosive of it.

These trends would have necessitated a serious rethinking of approaches to ownership, control and sponsorship of institutional apostolates even if the Second Vatican Council had not occurred.

[7] See Paul D. Starr, *The Social Transformation of American Medicine* (New York: Basic Books, 1982).

First Responses to the Unraveling: McGrath v. Maida

The beginnings of a shift in patterns of ownership, control and sponsorship of institutional apostolates in the United States can be traced to the 1960s and 1970s when religious institutes embarked on the program of separately incorporating their institutional apostolates and thereby giving these apostolates civil identities distinct from those of the sponsoring religious bodies. The immediate impetus for separate incorporation of institutional apostolates was to enhance their eligibility for government funding and to insulate the sponsoring religious body from liability for claims against the apostolate. However, this shift in corporate structure was often conducted under the banner of the so-called "McGrath thesis."[8] In essence, McGrath held that, when institutional apostolates are civilly incorporated, they acquire identities separate, both civilly and canonically, from those of their religious sponsors. Therefore, the property of these sponsored apostolates is no longer "church property" subject to the regulatory norms of canon law and these institutions themselves are governed solely by the norms of civil law, except to the extent that their state-recognized charters and by-laws incorporate a role for the religious sponsor in corporate governance.[9] The "McGrath thesis" became for some a sort of declaration of independence of institutional apostolates from church authority in general and canon law in particular.

The "McGrath thesis" soon evoked a sharply critical response from (then Father) Adam Maida.[10] Maida effectively refuted McGrath's claim that separate civil incorporation of institutional apostolates severed their canonical bond to their sponsoring religious entity. Thus, neither civil incorporation in itself nor changes in the structure and composition of governing boards has any canonical effect on the relationship between the religious sponsor and its institutional apostolate. Even after its separate civil incorporation, the property of these apostolates remains church property subject to the regulatory norms of canon law and the apostolates themselves fall under ecclesiastical as well as civil jurisdiction. Maida went on to advance the rather dubious argument that these institutional apostolates were themselves moral persons (now, public juridic persons) in the Church and, therefore, fully subject to canonical

[8] See John J. McGrath, *Catholic Institutions in the United States: Canonical and Civil Law Status* (Washington, DC: The Catholic University of America Press, 1968).
[9] Ibid., 24.
[10] Adam J. Maida, *Ownership, Control and Sponsorship of Catholic Institutions: A Practical Guide* (Harrisburg, Pa: Pennsylvania Catholic Conference, 1975).

regulation.[11] Nevertheless, Maida's fundamental argument that civil incorporation does not per se alter the canonical status of institutional apostolates and their property is sound. It articulates the position repeatedly put forward by the Apostolic See, which has consistently rejected the "McGrath thesis" and its corollaries, most recently in connection with the sale of the hospital of Saint Louis University to a for-profit chain.[12]

Nevertheless, the actual status of the property of many sponsored institutional apostolates in the United States is rather more complicated than either the "McGrath thesis" or the "Maida antithesis" would suggest. If

> it may fairly be said that McGrath oversimplified a complex matter by concluding that virtually no separately incorporated Catholic institution is subject to the laws of the Church governing ecclesiastical juridic persons, it seems equally fair to say that Maida also oversimplifies by concluding that all such institutions are so subject.[13]

In particular, Maida's conclusion does not adequately take into account the existence of some institutional apostolates that were founded as civil corporations under the general influence or inspiration of a diocese or religious institute

[11] For an analysis and critique of this second argument, see Robert T. Kennedy, "McGrath, Maida, Michiels: Introduction to a Study of the Canonical and Civil Law Status of Church Related Institutions in the United States," *The Jurist* 50 (1990) 377-399.

[12] On October 7, 1974, in a letter to the president of CMSM, the prefects of the Congregations for Catholic Education and for Religious and Secular Institutes insisted: "We know that in the course of the study, the influence of the so-called 'McGrath thesis' will emerge as one of the principal bases for the action of some institutions in regard to alienation, etc. We wish to make it clear that this thesis has never been considered valid by our Congregations and has never been accepted." *Roman Replies 1982*, ed. William Schumacher (Washington, DC: CLSA, 1982) 8. More recently, in a letter of January 28, 1998 to Father Hans Peter Hans- Kolvenbach, Superior General of the Society of Jesus, concerning the proposed sale of Saint Louis University Hospital, the prefects of the Congregation for Institutes of Consecrated Life and Societies of Apostolic Life and for Catholic Education again rejected the substance of the "McGrath thesis" without mentioning it explicitly: "The authorization of the Holy See is necessary for the sale of the Saint Louis University Hospital since the provisions of 1967 of appointing a self-perpetuating board of trustees, a majority of whom are not members of the Missouri Province of the Society of Jesus, did not constitute an alienation of ecclesiastical goods, whose owner, canonically considered, remains the Missouri province of the Society of Jesus as public juridic person of the church, and therefore the properties pertaining to Saint Louis University are still to be considered ecclesiastical goods." In Justin Rigali, "Saint Louis University Hospital Sold to For-Profit Corporation," *Origins* 27 (March 12, 1998) 631. For a fuller discussion of the Saint Louis University Hospital sale, see Daniel C. Conlin, *Canonical and Civil Legal Issues Surrounding the Alienation of Catholic Health Care Facilities in the United States* (Rome: Pontifical University of Saint Thomas, 2000) 174-178.

[13] Kennedy, "McGrath, Maida, Michiels," 377.

but that never shared the canonical status of the sponsoring body. Nor does Maida's position consider the possibility that, at the time of or subsequent to the separate incorporation of an institutional apostolate, the sponsoring juridic person conveyed property to the civil corporation with the intention of alienating it or that, since the separate incorporation, the institutional apostolate has acquired property from governmental or private donors whose clear intent was to benefit, not the sponsoring institute, but the incorporated apostolate.[14]

> Efforts to ascertain the present canonical status of a Catholic institution in the United States, therefore, should avoid misleading assumptions about the supposed canonical effects of civil law incorporation (or other civil-law structuring) of the institution, or changes in the composition of the institution's board of trustees, or transfers of civil title to real estate. Efforts should concentrate on careful research to determine the original canonical status of the institution and whether or not valid canonical steps were ever taken to alter that original status.[15]

Once the actual canonical status of an institutional apostolate has been ascertained, it is possible to weigh the advantages and disadvantages of other possible statuses and to take the appropriate canonical and civil steps to achieve the status most desirable in the light of all the present and foreseeable circumstances.

Weaving Bonds of Communion: The Place of Canon Law

Preoccupation with the question of the ownership of property has, unfortunately, fostered the erroneous view that, if the property of an institutional apostolate is not church property, i.e, property owned by some public juridic person in the Church (c. 1257, §1), then canon law is wholly irrelevant to the apostolate's operations. This preoccupation has also fostered the equally erroneous view that, unless an apostolic institution is owned by some public juridic person in the Church and is fully subject to all of the provisions of canon law, especially those governing the administration and alienation of ecclesiastical goods, it is not authentically Catholic. The mistaken identification of ownership of property with effective institutional control seems to be one of the "lessons" learned

[14] Ibid., 370-377.

[15] Robert T. Kennedy, "Note on the Canonical Status of Church-Related Institutions in the United States," in *A New Commentary on the Code of Canon Law*, ed. John P. Beal, et. al. (Mahwah, NJ: Paulist Press, 2000) 176.

by church authorities in the United States from the "lay trustee controversy" of the nineteenth century. In that conflict, the bishops discovered that the most efficient way to make their authority felt in parishes and to secure recognition of their episcopal authority from the secular courts was to wrest ownership of parish property from the lay trustees. The bitterness engendered by this controversy left a lingering suspicion that undertakings not wholly owned and controlled by some hierarchical authority in the Church were only inauthentically "Catholic."[16] Nevertheless, numerous Catholic associations for charitable and religious purposes have flourished and maintained communion with the Church without their property ever being church property regulated by canon law. No one has recently accused the Saint Vincent DePaul Society, the Knights of Columbus, or the Catholic Worker, none of which is owned or sponsored by a public juridic person, of being deficient in its Catholicity.[17] Wrangling about the ownership of property of institutional apostolates can be–and sometimes has been–a distraction from the more critical task of maintaining and strengthening the Catholic identity of these apostolates.

Since they are in the communion of the Church, all Catholics, both individually and joined together in associations, are bound by canon law, to paraphrase Cole Porter, "after their fashion;" however, their status in the Church determines which of these laws bind (and do not bind) them. Institutional apostolates can exist in the Church in a variety of juridically recognized forms. They can take the form of independent public juridic persons, wholly owned subsidiaries of some public juridic person, private juridic persons, public or private associations, or even de facto associations. Each of these forms has different requirements for canonical recognition and is regulated differently by canon law, but all of them are subject to canon law in some way. At the very least, all the faithful, regardless of their status or condition, are bound "to maintain communion with the Church," whether they act as individuals or in association with others (c. 209, §1). "Maintaining communion" is not merely a matter of having a vague but affectionate feeling for the Church in general or an undefined respect for the pope or the local bishop. Rather, as the Second Vatican Council said of that special form of communion which binds bishops to the Head of the College of Bishops and its members, communion is understood

[16] John P. Beal, "The Inculturation of Canon Law: Made in the USA," *Concilium* (1996/5) 50-51. See Patrick W. Carey, *People, Priests, and Prelates: Ecclesiastical Democracy and the Tensions of Trusteeism* (Notre Dame, IN: University of Notre Dame Press, 1987).

[17] On the relative autonomy of the Saint Vincent DePaul Society within the Church and its immunity from the laws governing church property, see Sacred Congregation for the Council, resolution, November 14, 1920: *CLD* 1: 714-715.

"not of a certain vague feeling, but of an *organic reality* which demands a juridical form, and is simultaneously animated by charity."[18] While this organic reality of communion can be manifested in a wide variety of forms, it requires of its very nature the forging, maintaining, and strengthening of visible bonds of communion between the institutional apostolate and the larger Church out of whose heart it was born on the one hand and between this larger Church and the institutional apostolate on the other. Canon law serves the Church and institutional apostolates in the Church by defining and clarifying the criteria for the recognition of institutional apostolates in and by the Church and articulating the rights and responsibilities of these apostolates in the Church and of the Church toward these apostolates.

Forging and maintaining bonds of communion between the Church and institutional apostolates in the Church entails responsibilities both for the apostolates themselves and for the Church, especially its hierarchical leadership. Much of the discussion of the role of the Church's hierarchical authorities in maintaining communion with apostolates has focused on the right and responsibility of these authorities to intervene and regulate when the bonds of communion become frayed. Too little attention has been devoted to articulating the positive responsibilities for fostering and promoting these apostolic institutions on the part of Church leadership. On the part of institutional apostolates, these bonds of communion entail: the establishment and maintenance of a mutually recognized relationship with the Church's hierarchical leadership, adherence to the Church's teaching in the institution's operations and activities, and an institutional commitment to embedding the founding charism in the institution's daily life.

A Bond of Communion with the Church's Hierarchy

As apostolates "in the Church," health care, education and charitable institutions are necessarily in communion with the Church's hierarchical leadership. This communion requires some juridic expression and recognition, but this juridic expression can take a variety of forms, some of which involve the ownership of the apostolates' property by a public juridic person and some of which do not.

[18] Vatican II, dogmatic constitution Lumen Gentium, November 21, 1964: *AAS* 56(1965)5-67, *Nota explicativa praevia*, 2.

The Sponsor as Owner-Operator

This communion between the apostolate and the Church was so clear that it was rarely mentioned when the traditional model of sponsorship of institutional apostolates by religious institutes or dioceses prevailed. In this traditional model, the sponsoring public juridic person owned the property of its apostolic institution and through this ownership exercised control over its direction and operations. However, ownership of property is only one factor–and not necessarily the most important factor–in insuring that the institutional apostolate continues to carry out its evangelical purpose in and out of the heart of the Church. Ownership of the institutional apostolate's property by a public juridic person in the Church can enable the public juridic person, through its lawful representatives, to influence, monitor, and, if need be, control the direction and activities of the sponsored apostolate. Ownership may provide legal leverage for exerting influence, but ownership alone does not guarantee that the influence, monitoring, and control which ownership makes possible will be exercised or exercised effectively. Absentee ownership's loss of effective control of an institution is not a problem found exclusively in the secular world. The historical example of institutional apostolates of other churches and religious groups which have drifted slowly but inexorably out of the sphere of control and influence of the sponsoring body even as the sponsoring denomination retained ownership of the apostolate's property is a cautionary reminder that ownership alone is no guarantee of religious identity.[19] It is perhaps for this reason that John Paul II was able to devote the whole of his apostolic constitution *Ex corde Ecclesiae* to the criteria for Catholic identity of colleges and universities without even once adverting to the issue of ownership of the institutions' property.

Sponsor as Corporate Conscience

Perhaps in recognition of the need for something more than the mere ownership of property to insure the continued Catholic identity of institutional apostolates, many canonical sponsors have restructured their relationships with sponsored institutions through the device of a membership corporation

[19] See George Marsden, *The Soul of the American University: From Protestant Establishment to Established Non-Belief* (New York: Oxford, 1994) and James Tunstead Burtchaell, *The Dying of the Light: The Disengagement of Colleges and Universities from their Christian Churches* (Grand Rapids, MI: Eerdmans, 1998). For a somewhat more sanguinary perspective, see Robert A. Armour, "American Higher Education and the Churches: A United Methodist Perspective on Catholic Identity and Methodist Ethos," *The Jurist* 59 (1999) 98-110.

in which responsibility for the day to day management of the institution is vested in the chief executive officer and the board of trustees but in which the canonical sponsor enjoys certain reserved powers over the direction and philosophy of the institution. Most commentators agree that, to exert meaningful control over its institutional apostolate, a sponsor needs to reserve at least the powers:

1) to establish the philosophy according to which the corporation operates,
2) to amend the corporate charter and by laws,
3) to appoint or approve the appointment of the board of trustees,
4) to sell, lease, or encumber corporate real estate in excess of the approved sum, and
5) to merge or dissolve the corporation.[20]

More recently, at least in the field of health care, sponsors have enhanced their efforts "to monitor the implementation of mission values in the corporation's governance, management, and service."[21]

This shift in emphasis in discussions of sponsorship away from property ownership and management toward mission effectiveness entails at least a tacit recognition that ownership of the property of an institutional apostolate does not automatically translate into the control of its philosophy and culture needed to integrate the eloquent prose of mission statements into the sometimes gritty everyday operations of the institution. However, it needs to be remembered that even the reservation of extensive powers to the sponsoring agency will not insure mission fidelity, much less mission effectiveness, unless the sponsors can deploy enough competent personnel (not necessarily all members of the sponsoring body) sufficiently engaged in the operation of the institutional apostolate to exercise these reserved powers effectively. Otherwise, the aegis of sponsorship by a religious organization and programs for mission effectiveness will be little more than attractive wrapping paper for an institution that is no more distinctively Catholic or redolent of the charism of the sponsoring religious body than Wal-Mart. Already, there is concern expressed

[20] The Catholic Health Association of the United States, *The Search for Identity: Canonical Sponsorship of Catholic Healthcare* (Saint Louis, MO: CHA, 1993) 81. Similar but somewhat longer lists of reserved powers are suggested in Francis Morrisey, "Basic Concepts and Principles," in *Church Finance Handbook*, ed. Kevin McKenna, et al. (Washington, DC: CLSA, 1999) 14 and Adam Maida and Nicholas Cafardi, *Church Property, Church Finances, and Church-Related Corporations* (Saint Louis, MO: CHA, 1984) 167-169.

[21] CHA, *The Search for Identity*, 44.

in the field of Catholic health care that "mission is no longer the guiding focus of organizational decisions but rather is considered after survival–and possibly even growth–strategies have been considered."[22] Similar concerns have been voiced about the perceived marginalization of mission related concerns in educational institutions.[23]

Alternative Sponsorship Models

The sharp decline in the number of religious, especially women religious, competent and available to exercise their institute's sponsorship responsibilities toward institutional apostolates has prompted considerable discussion of alternative models of sponsorship, including transfer of these sponsorship responsibilities and reserved powers from the founding religious institute to diocesan bishops and even to public and private associations of the faithful. Although most experiments with alternative sponsorship models have occurred in the field of health care, they are not unknown in the field of education, especially at the level of elementary and secondary schools. Implicit in the discussion of sponsorship models, reserved powers and monitoring mission effectiveness is a recognition that the Catholic identity of institutional apostolates is not something given once and for all but a goal that must be maintained and fostered, something that requires committed leadership both from within the institution and from outside it.

> Ultimately, there is in fact no panacea, no silver bullet, no once-and-for-all solution to insure Catholic identity.... [N]o one thing will do it, but rather constant alertness to opportunities, initiatives on many fronts, with some successes, some failures, no quitting. None of this can be accomplished without leadership. That means presidents of Catholic colleges and universities who don't make Catholic identity an afterthought but rank it with the top concerns (primarily financial) that daily occupy their attention. That also means second-tier and middle-level staff in administration and faculties who do not view fostering their [institution's] Catholic identity as a burden–or as someone else's task–but as a challenge to be creative and reflective.[24]

[22] Marie Wolff, "No Margin, No Mission: Challenge to Institutional Ethics," *Business and Professional Ethics Journal* 12 (Summer, 1993) 45.

[23] See Peter Steinfels, *A People Adrift: The Crisis of the Roman Catholic Church in America* (New York: Simon and Schuster, 2003) 131-161.

[24] Steinfels, 160.

Even such leadership is unlikely to be effective unless some identifiable and stable group, passionately and doggedly committed to the apostolate's identity and mission, is responsible for maintaining and fostering this Catholic identity. The canonical status of this cadre is less important than its commitment, its legal authority over and within the institution, and its ability to sustain and perpetuate itself. Otherwise, Catholic identity is likely to fade with the passing of the founding members or the withdrawal from active participation by the sponsor. Canon law can serve these institutional apostolates that have arisen out of the heart of the Church by identifying those responsible for fostering their Catholic identity, delineating their rights and responsibilities, and holding them accountable for their fulfillment.

A Bond of Communion in Faith

A second bond of communion between an institutional apostolate and the larger Church is the apostolate's institutional commitment to adhering to the Church's doctrinal and moral teaching both in its official documents and in its day-to-day operations. Indeed, Catholic apostolic institutions historically have been and must continue to be prophetic voices in the educational, health care, and social service market places. For health care facilities, institutional adherence to Church teaching usually takes the form of incorporation of the "Ethical and Religious Directives for Catholic Health Care Facilities" issued by the United States Conference of Catholic Bishops into their governing documents.[25] For Catholic colleges and universities, it takes the form of commitment to compliance with the implementing norms for *Ex corde Ecclesiae*, including their provision for those who teach theology and related disciplines to seek a mandatum from the diocesan bishop of the place where the institution is located.[26] While it may be impossible for an institutional apostolate to be recognized as, or even to be, Catholic without institutional adherence to the teaching on faith and morals proposed by the Magisterium, incorporation of statements of such adherence into its corporate documents and promotional literature will not insure its Catholic identity. By proscribing certain procedures

[25] United States Conference of Catholic Bishops, *Ethical and Religious Directives for Catholic Health Care Services* (Washington, DC: USCC, 2001).

[26] United States Conference of Catholic Bishops, "The Application of *Ex corde Ecclesiae* for the United States," *Origins* 30 (June 15, 2000) 68-75 and Id., *Guidelines Concerning the Academic Mandatum in Catholic Universities* (Washington, DC: USCC, 2001).

and treatments as incompatible with magisterial teaching, the "Ethical and Religious Directives" define what Catholic health care facilities must not do. However, equal attention needs to be paid to what these directives have to say about what sort of care Catholic facilities ought to provide and what sort of institutions they ought to be. Similarly, the orthodoxy of the members of theological faculty of an educational institution will have little impact, for good or ill, on the Catholic character of their institution when, for example, students take only two theology courses during their four years of matriculation or the theology faculty itself is a lonely island cut off from the rest of academia. Institutional professions of orthodoxy cannot substitute for vibrant, living faith within the institution.

Internal Bonds of Communion

To sustain and foster the Catholic identity of institutional apostolates, the bonds of communion that keep these apostolic undertakings firmly rooted in the larger Church need to be complemented by internal bonds that draw the individuals and constituencies who participate in the institution's apostolate into communion with one another for the sake of their common ecclesial mission. Communitarian rhetoric pervades the mission statements and governance documents of institutional apostolates, but this rhetoric often rings hollow when confronted with reality. It is hard to imagine institutions more impervious to communitarian trends than contemporary hospitals. In addition to the centrifugal effect of ever greater specialization in the medical profession, hospitals are often rigidly stratified institutions with little upward or downward mobility. Administrators, trustees, medical staff, nurses, technicians, housekeeping and maintenance personnel, and others, all cling tightly and, at times, protectively to their group's place in the operation. Fostering communities of service in such caste-ridden institutions is a daunting challenge, a challenge that many Catholic institutions have begun to address with some promising results. Only slightly less daunting is the challenge of promoting a genuine community of teachers and learners in educational institutions, especially institutions of higher education, with their own caste systems and internecine "turf" wars.

Nevertheless, maintenance of Catholic identity demands that those responsible for apostolic institutions accept the ongoing challenge of forging and fostering bonds of communion within their institutions. To meet this challenge requires institutional commitments to developing and implementing effective programs of formation for all participants in the institutions apostolic work, pursuing social justice, providing pastoral care, and demonstrating concern for the poor.

1. In all institutional apostolates, maintaining Catholic identity requires more than Catholic language in mission statements and corporate documents. Catholic identity cannot be successfully imposed on an institution from outside and cannot be guaranteed by outsiders, whether they are bishops or leaders of the sponsoring religious institute, but must grow organically from within. What John Paul II said of Catholic universities is also applicable to other institutional apostolates: "The responsibility for maintaining and strengthening the Catholic identity of the university rests primarily with the university itself. While this responsibility is entrusted principally to university authorities..., it is shared in varying degrees by all members of the university community."[27] Catholic identity depends, therefore, on the presence of a "critical mass" of strategically situated participants in the institution's apostolic ministry who are dedicated to its redemptive ministry and see their participation in that mission as something more than a job. It was priests and religious who often provided this "critical mass" in the past; lay people alone or in concert with religious will have to provide it in the future. It is hard to see how that "critical mass" can develop within the institution unless the leadership is committed to "hiring for mission."[28] The critical challenge facing institutional apostolates today is that of developing and implementing effective formation programs for lay leaders and participants in the institutions ministry.
2. The credibility of the Church's proclamation of the Gospel is undermined when its own internal life, including that of its institutional apostolates, does not mirror the justice it preaches. Catholic institutional apostolates need to be attentive to the demands of social justice when they make decisions about what services and programs to offer and how and where to allocate their resources. These decisions should be made in light of the real needs of the communities they serve rather than of merely financial considerations. The Church's social teaching must also inform employer-employee relations in these institutions. It will be difficult to convince employees to treat their jobs as a participation in a ministry, if the term "ministry" is used to "candy-coat" substandard

[27] John Paul II, apostolic constitution *Ex corde Ecclesiae*, art. 4, §1.
[28] See Steinfels, 151-160.

wages, lack of job security, and unsatisfactory working conditions. In their 1986 pastoral letter on Catholic social teaching and the economy, the bishops of the United States insisted: "*All the moral principles that govern the just operation of any economic endeavor apply to the Church and its agencies and institutions; indeed the Church should be exemplary.*"[29]

3. If their efforts at formation of participants in their mission are to take root and flourish, institutional apostolates need to be committed to seeing that adequate pastoral care is provided. This commitment entails making adequate provision for departments of pastoral services in health care institutions and campus ministry in educational institutions. The scope of this pastoral care should extend not just to the beneficiaries of the institutional apostolate's ministry but also to those who carry out its ministry. Thus, hospital departments of pastoral care should be attentive to the spiritual needs of hospital personnel as well of patients and their families, and campus ministries should direct their programs not only to students but also to faculty and staff. The pastoral care provided in institutional apostolates is not simply a substitute for the pastoral care people normally receive in the parishes from which they are temporarily absent, but an integral part of the life and mission of the institution. Speaking of Catholic colleges and universities, John Paul II noted: "Pastoral ministry is that activity of the university which offers the members of the university community an opportunity to integrate religious and moral principles with their academic study and non-academic activities, thus *integrating faith and life*."[30] This effort at integration of faith and life should be the hallmark of the pastoral care provided in and through all institutional apostolates.

4. "Preferential option for the poor" has become something of a mantra in Catholic circles in recent years. However, translating that mantra into the daily praxis of institutional apostolates has become increasingly problematic as the commodification of health care, education, and many of the other services they provide has become more pervasive. The prospering and, at times, even the survival of these apostolates often depends on decisions made with an eye more to their impact on the "bottom line" than on their impact on the poor. Aggressive cost containment measures by third party insurers has made it impossible for health care facilities to pass along the cost of care for the indigent to paying customers and thus has

[29] National Conference of Catholic Bishops, *Economic Justice for All: Pastoral Letter on Catholic Social Teaching and the U.S. Economy* (Washington, DC: USCC, 1986) §347. Emphasis in the original.
[30] John Paul II, apostolic constitution *Ex corde Ecclesiae*, §38. Emphasis in the original.

sharply limited the amount of charity care the facilities' budgets can absorb. Educational institutions need to attract enough students who can pay rising tuitions so that they can pay decent salaries to an almost exclusively lay faculty and staff and offer the programs and amenities which will keep them competitive in the market for student-consumers. While institutional apostolates cannot stand Canute-like against the tide of a consumerist culture, they can commit themselves to respecting the dignity of the poor they do serve by giving them the same quality of care or education and the same personal attention that they give to the better-off. Decisions about where to locate (or re-locate) facilities, which types of services and programs to provide or discontinue, and what sort of equipment to purchase can be made in the light of their impact on the poor. Catholic health care facilities can also advocate vigorously on behalf of public policies designed to insure more equitable access to health care for the poor, and Catholic educational institutions can sensitize their students to the needs of the poor and incorporate Catholic social teaching into the curriculum not only in theology classes but in other academic areas. An institutional apostolate that cannot make a credible case for its efforts to translate the preferential option for the poor from slogan into substance may have no justification for continued existence.

Conclusion

Apostolic institutions in the Church have had a stormy journey through the decades since the Second Vatican Council. Buffeted by the ecclesiological gales stemming from the council itself and caught in the eddy of societal forces over which they had no control, these apostolic institutions have tossed and turned on seas of troubles. In these turbulent seas, some of these institutions have sunk, but most remain afloat. In the years ahead, there is no reason to think the waves of upheaval will be calmed or the winds of change less fierce. To stay not only afloat but on course during the coming storms, these institutions will have to identify and develop competent and visionary leaders who can find within their institutions themselves the material and spiritual resources needed to allow their ministry not merely to survive but to flourish and who can mobilize the Church to works of the apostolate and charity that are central to its own identity and mission. Success in this endeavor is not assured, but who would have predicted success from Jesus' program of sending out his first disciples two by two.

CHAPTER FOUR

Sponsorship By Juridic Persons

WILLIAM J. KING

Students of Catholic theology often quip that the correct answer to any difficult exam question is "the Paschal mystery," since, in a rather cosmic sense, all of theology finds its root in that singular event. In a similar vein, many questions of contemporary canon law can be answered with the utterance, "*communio*." Many of the structures and provisions of canon law are directly in service of the reality represented by the theological principle of *communio*, and it is the hallmark and guarantee of an authentically Catholic approach to legal implementation and apostolic endeavor.

Prospectus

This brief look at sponsorship by juridic persons will begin by looking at one aspect of the theological/canonical principle of *communio* – an aspect grounded in the roots of the word itself. Following this, we will examine the notion of a "juridic person" and its place in the canonical menagerie of corporate structures. Third, we will briefly lay out some of the principal distinctions between *public* and *private* juridic persons. Fourth, we will consider the establishment of a juridic person. Fifth, some supporting notions in theory and practice will be presented. Finally, several criteria or indicators for choosing between public and private will be offered, followed by a general summary.

A Theological Context: Building the City of God

In order to enter a discussion of "sponsorship by juridic persons," it may be helpful to construct the broad vision of *communio* itself, as a precursor to examining the legal structures of juridic personality.

To that end, it is interesting to note the common etymology of two words: *munus* and *communio*. Deriving from the archaic Latin word *moenio*, these words refer back in some way to the concept of a fortifying wall erected for the protection of citizens of a town, city, or village. The wall of the city served two purposes: a defense against enemies, and a definition of space for commercial and governmental enterprise. The wall both protected those within, and invited or enhanced collaboration among residents. In turn, the commerce of a city or town invited new craftsmen, traders, consumers, and citizens.

As the word *moenio* evolved by usage into *munio* to describe the wall, the term municeps came to designate an inhabitant of a walled town or city, and the area within the walls (the *municipium*) evolved into the modern word municipality. The verb munire indicates the building up or fortification of a wall for defense ("munition" and "ammunition" derive from this meaning), and the task or duty of all citizens to assist in the building and maintenance of the wall is described as a munus. The adjectival form, munis, indicating one who is ready to be of service, defines the willingness and preparedness to assist in the common maintenance and fortification of the city's wall. The word "ministry" is a direct descendent of this adjective, munis, indicating a willingness to be of service. Mutual participation in the task of maintaining the wall came to be known as *communio*, and the verb *communire* or working together toward the common defense means "to fortify on all sides or strongly, to secure, barricade, intrench."[1]

Why is this foray into Latin etymology important to understanding juridic personality in canon law? Not only do juridical structures and institutes such as the "juridic person" serve to reinforce the *communio* of the Church, but one of the essential distinctions among juridic persons is the conferral of a *munus* by ecclesiastical authority. Understanding the history of this term allows one to understand that the conferral of a *munus* on a juridic person inserts it into the public order of the Church, and connects it to the common purpose of building up or fortifying the "walls" of the Church in a certain symbolic, even mystical, sense. It is not a stretch of theological language to connect the

[1] C.T. Lewis, *A Latin Dictionary*, Oxford 1879.

conferral of a *munus* to the building up of the Heavenly City referred to in the book of Revelation (Rev. 21:2 ff.). The maintenance of *communio* in the Church is directly related to the twofold purpose of a wall for an ancient city-state: to fortify and defend the work of a common citizenship, and to protect, encourage, and enable the commerce of the city.

Both functions of *communio* are important in our common citizenship in the Heavenly City. In the litigious environment of our earthly realm, choice of legal structures to define sponsorship, governance, and ownership, is still related to protecting the City of God from the unloving, and hence a *munus* still demands collaboration with our fellow citizens toward a common defense and common protective nurturing of apostolic activity. The apostolate or ministry of the Church is the commerce of the Heavenly City, into which we, by a successful fostering of *communion*, invite others. Successful *communio* nurtures the works of the Church as leaven in the modern world.

Although a great deal more may be said about the meaning and significance of *communio* in the context of sponsorship and sponsored ministries, it will suffice to note that the preservation of *communio* among persons, organizations, institutions and groups in large measure determines the choice of structures and the drafting of legal provisions which define the sponsor relationship. This is especially true when the juridical structure for the sponsorship relationship is that of the juridic person, since the distinction between a public juridic person and a private juridic person is essentially whether it fulfills a *munus* in the name of the Church or, instead, fulfills a mission in its own name. In sweeping terms, the distinction is the degree of participation of the organization and its activities in the overall life and ministry of the Church itself, but more about this will be discussed below.

The Notion of a Juridic Person

The *Code of Canon Law* of 1983 notes tersely, "In the Church, besides physical persons, there are also juridic persons, that is, subjects in canon law of obligations and rights which correspond to their nature."[2] The Code continues, "...they are aggregates of persons or of things ordered for a purpose which is in keeping with the mission of the Church and which transcends the purpose of the individuals."[3] These simple declarations belie a lengthy historical development.

[2] Canon 113, §2

[3] Canon 114, §1

Historical Review

Along with esoteric questions concerning the divinity of Christ, the reality of the Incarnation, and the nature of the Blessed Trinity, the early Church also faced more gritty issues such as ownership and control of properties and monies given to the Church. Within the first century of Christianity, there was a growing understanding that temporal goods given to the Church were set aside for the ministries of the Church[4] and their administration was in the hands of the bishop, though distinct from his personal possessions.[5] By the third century the existence of ecclesiastical property was generally recognized.[6] In a simple and unreflective manner, it came to be accepted that some means or principle of ownership existed distinct from both the individual members of the Church as well as the person of the bishop.

As law developed within the Church, including canonical institutes of property tenure and ecclesiastical governance, two parallel realms of ownership and apostolic activity developed: that of the territorial or particular church – the diocese – and that of the Religious Orders or Institutes of Consecrated Life (as evolved from the loosely-articulated groupings of monks in early centuries into the well-defined Orders of the high Middle Ages). Side-by-side with these truly "ecclesiastical" modes of temporal ownership and governance, there emerged groups of like-minded individuals who collaborated to assist each other in spiritual or charitable works, or to promote wider practice of works of mercy. These gave historical root to what are now called "associations of the faithful,"[7] whereas the more formal models of governance and ownership are currently known as "juridic persons." The distinction between associations of the faithful and juridic persons is discussed below, but this historical review is important as the concepts of sponsorship and sponsored ministries apply equally to those of dioceses, to those of institutes of consecrated life, and to

[4] Cf. B.F. Brown, *The Canonical Juristic Personality with Special References to Its Status in the United States of America*, Canon Law Studies 39, Washington DC, 28-29. Cf. also C.J. Hefele, *A History of the Councils of the Church, from the Original Documents*, in which canons 24 and 25 of the Synod of Antioch are translated at page 73; or J.D. Mansi, *Sacrorum Conciliorum Nova et Amplissima Collectio*, in which the same canons are presented at column 1335.

[5] Cf. *Apostolic Constitutions*, 31, 34, 37; and *Apostolic Constitutions* Book II, cc. 25, 27, 35.

[6] Brian E. Ferme, "The Temporal Goods of the Church: Some Historical Notes and Reflections," in Joseph Fox, *Render unto Caesar: Church Property in Roman Catholic and Anglican Canon Law*, 9-10.

[7] Cf. A. García y García, "Significación del Elemento Asociativo en la Historia del Derecho de la Iglesia," in *Das Konsoziative Element in Der Kirche, Achte Des VI Internationalen Kongresses Für Kanonischen Recht, München 14-19 September 1987*, München 1987; and also John R. Amos, *Associations of the Faithful in the 1983 Code of Canon Law: A Canonical Analysis and Evaluation*, Washington DC, 1986.

those of associations of the faithful. Property tenure and governance can be exercised by legally-enacted ministries of any of the three.

Legal development of the juridic person continued apace into the Renaissance and modern era. Influenced by the early codifications of secular law in the states of continental Europe, the first codification of law in the Catholic Church – the 1917 *Code of Canon Law* (which pertained to the Latin Rite church only) – contained the notion of a "moral person." Book II of that Code, *De Personis*, treated of persons in the Church. Canons 99 through 106 concerned moral persons. Canon 99 provided, "In the Church, besides physical persons there are also moral persons, constituted by public authority, which are distinguished into collegial and non-collegial moral persons..." The distinction between *collegial* and *non-collegial* was principally whether the legal reality consisted of a "college" of physical persons, or, instead, of a collection of "...property and resources... dedicated to some religious and charitable purpose."[8] A collegiate moral person was also referred to as a "corporative" moral person, and a non-collegiate moral person was called an "institutional" moral person.[9]

The 1983 *Code of Canon Law* continues to provide for a structure of ownership and governance of property distinct from individuals within the Church.[10] What were formerly called "moral persons" are now called "juridic persons," designating their origin in a provision of law or a legal enactment.[11] The distinction remains, as in the earlier Code, between those juridic persons which are essentially groups of persons and those which are a collection of property or assets dedicated to a purpose related to religion or charity. However, this is no longer the principal distinction between juridic persons. Rather, the 1983 Code proposed a new high-order distinction: that of the *public* and *private* juridic person.

[8] Gomarus Michiels, *Principia Generale de Personis in Ecclesia*, 355.

[9] *Ibid.*, 355.

[10] The 1990 *Code of Canons of the Eastern Churches* treats of juridic persons in its canons 920-930. It is interesting to note that this "Eastern Code" does not contain the distinction between public and private juridic persons, but does contain a bit more specificity regarding what is necessary in the statutes of juridic persons. The Eastern Code provides for associations of the faithful in its canons 573-583, there containing the distinction between public and private.

[11] The 1983 *Code of Canon Law* continues to use the term "moral person" to denote those entities which exist prior to and apart from any operation of the law, specifically the Catholic Church and the Apostolic See (canon 113).

Associations of the Faithful and Juridic Persons in the 1983 Code

This distinction parallels that made among *associations of the faithful*, another institute of the 1983 *Code of Canon Law*. Associations of the faithful also may be either public or private.[12] In the drafting of the 1983 Code, the evolution of both associations of the faithful and juridic persons began together, but they were later separated as the drafting progressed. It can be seen that the law of the Church makes a distinction between *associations of the faithful and juridic persons*.[13] The two are parallel but not identical.

What are the differences between an association of the faithful and a juridic person? It may be said that the primary elements of *associations of the faithful* are the charismatic and associative elements, and that the primary elements of *juridic persons* are the institutional and property elements. While this distinction is not entirely accurate (it is far too vague), it does steer us toward an understanding of what distinguishes an association of the faithful from a juridic person. Historically, associations of the faithful emerge from the desire to foster either the practice of the corporal works of mercy or the spiritual life among their members. Juridic persons historically emerge from the need to define property ownership and accountability. A goal of juridic personality is to ensure the means for continuance of the work.

Juridic personality achieves a legal identity at canon law apart from the founders, a legal identity which continues after they or the current members are gone; an association of the faithful, however, cannot be thought of as existing apart from the persons who make it up. Hence, canon 310 of the 1983 *Code of Canon Law* observes:

> A private association which has not been constituted a juridic person cannot as such be a subject of obligations and rights; however, the Christian faithful associated together in it can jointly contract obligations and acquire rights and possess goods as co-owners and co-possessors; they can exercise their rights and obligations through an agent or proxy.

[12] Although some canonists will employ the term, *de facto association of the faithful* to denote such an association which has not received ecclesiastical approval, the commission drafting the 1983 *Code of Canon Law* explicitly rejected such a concept from inclusion among the categories of associations. The 1990 *Code of Canons of the Eastern Churches*, however, recognizes among *private* associations of the faithful those which have no ecclesiastical recognition or approbation.

[13] This distinction becomes apparent in considering the evolution of the texts in the process of drafting the 1983 Code. Cf. William J. King, *Public and Private Juridic Personality: A Comparative Legal Analysis*, JCD dissertation at the Pontifical Gregorian University, 2002, esp. pp. 43-70. Cf. also the reports published in *Communicationes* in the following volumes: 2(1970); 6(1974); 21(1989).

A juridic person, whether private or public, is a subject of obligations and rights apart from the individuals who comprise it; a juridic person can enter into contracts and hold title to property, real and moveable, apart from the individuals who comprise it; members and officers of a juridic person are not co-owners or joint tenants of the property of the juridic person and can claim no possessory interests on that basis alone; the legal rights and interests of a juridic person are exercised by its proper administrator. Clearly there are distinctions between an *association of the faithful* and a *juridic person.*

The 1983 Code does not lay out a coherent or systematic approach to associations of the faithful and juridic persons. There is no incremental path of development laid out, and no clear criteria for choosing between the two categories. In part, this is intentional: it was the desire of the drafters of the Code not to confine the work of the Holy Spirit in the life of God's people, and so wording was kept loose and structures were left without great specificity, in order to allow them to evolve.[14]

Associations of the Faithful may be public or private. In the drafting of the Code, this distinction was understood as whether the group is founded by ecclesiastical authority or upon the initiative of the Christian faithful. However, overlaid atop this simple distinction is the fact that a *public association of the faithful* becomes also, by law, a *public juridic person.*

Simplistically, the difference between an association of the faithful and a juridic person can be understood as the difference between, on one hand, persons cooperating to accomplish a task coherent with the values and mission of the Church, and on the other hand, the set of structures and resources which enable the task or mission to continue in theoretical perpetuity. There are, to be sure, layers of additional distinctions in theory and practice which separate associations from juridic persons, but at its heart the distinction is simple.

Not every undertaking of a Catholic or group of Catholics is a "Catholic" work, however. It is partly the service of the public authority of the Church, in hierarchical *communio,* to discern and identify for the larger community those works which are truly Catholic and authentically connected with the mission of the Church in the world. A group of Catholics may collaborate toward a common work without forming, or intending to form, an association of the faithful by their common undertaking. An association, just as a juridic person, requires

[14] This is made quite clear in *Communicationes* 21(1989)138, in which the coetus or commission working on these canons noted their desire to avoid a conflict between the "charismatic" and "legal" elements of the Church, and decided that the legal structures provided by the law should exist primarily to catalyze "the progressive participation of the faithful in the common and unique mission of the Church, which sojourns in this world: they are therefore not to be set up as obstacles..." [transl. by author].

that a juridic act by the public authority of the Church either recognize its existence or formally confer canonical existence. The drafters of the 1983 Code explicitly rejected the notion of a de facto association of the faithful.

Functions of Juridic Personality

Juridic personality is undertaken, in part, to provide for continuity, stability, and perpetuity in performing a religious or charitable work. Juridic personality includes assuming such burdens as defined fiscal controls and governance accountability structures. The status of juridic personality provides for property ownership to be distinct from the individuals who comprise or administer the juridic person or apostolic work, and partial insulation of the participating persons from canonical legal liability. The *Code of Canon Law* itself confers public juridic personality on certain institutions and groups to ensure their continuity in apostolic work and to distinguish their assets, obligations and rights from the individuals who comprise them: among these are parishes, dioceses, provinces of religious institutes, and seminaries.

The purpose of assuming the legal mantle of "juridic person" is multifold:

- to establish and maintain a clear institutional identity within the Church;
- to provide for property tenure by a legal entity distinct from individuals;
- to segregate assets under canon law from other legal entities;
- to certify fiscal controls and accountability.

By what terms, then, does canon law identify juridic persons? They are identified as aggregates of *persons* or of *things*, and *public* or *private* in character.

Aggregates of Persons or Things

Juridic persons may be aggregates of persons or of things. "Aggregate" is not a perfect translation of the Latin word *universitas*. However, it may be said that the "substrate" in reality for a juridic person may be either physical persons or material resources. It is not necessary for the establishment of a juridic person that its substrate be declared. That is to say that the document establishing the juridic person need not state whether it is an *universitas* of persons or of things. The *Code of Canon Law* makes this second-order distinction (second to the public-private distinction) in order to clarify that the matter for a juridic person may be either persons or material resources, unlike *associations of the faithful* which by definition must be comprised of persons.

An example of a juridic person which has not persons but material resources as its substrate or matter is an autonomous pious foundation in canon law, which may be a sum of money donated and dedicated to one or more functions of charity or religion. The foundation is overseen by one or more Trustees, but the matter which comprises the juridic person is the monetary sum. A parish or a province of a religious institute are examples of public juridic persons which are comprised of persons and not of material resources. The material resources of a parish or a religious institute assist the apostolic activities of its persons, but the parish or institute would still exist even if it lost all of its material resources. The same cannot be said of an *universitas rerum* or juridic person which has as its substrate material resources: if those resources were lost, the work of the juridic person would stop. In practice, especially for relationships of sponsorship in Catholic higher education and Catholic healthcare, the distinction is more academic than real, and may remain unspoken or unstated as the notion of sponsorship is given legal precision by a choice and description of structure under both civil and canon law.[15]

The Private and Public Distinction

The distinction which remains primary and most practical is that of private and public juridic personality. Two things distinguish *public* and *private* in this context: conferral by ecclesiastical authority of a *munus* and action *in the name of the Church*.[16] When both of these elements are present in the founding of a juridic person, it is a *public* juridic person; when one is lacking it is a *private* juridic person. Both concepts are related, yet they are not identical.

[15] It is interesting to note as well that the wording of the canon leaves open the possibility that an "aggregate of persons" may consist in its membership not of physical persons but of juridic persons. It is conceivable, then, that a juridic person may exist as a collaboration, or "holding company," of other juridic persons. A consortium of institutions may collaborate in such a way as to form collectively a juridic person in order to perform a joint endeavor or joint enterprise. Reasons for doing so may range from the simple desire to parallel the secular legal structures with canonical enactments, to the notion of isolating Catholic practices and institutions within an even larger system of providers or delivery of services, to the goal of increasing the perceived Catholic identity of a joint enterprise or consortium of similar service providers.

[16] Canon 116 reads: "§1. Public juridic persons are aggregates of persons or things which are so constituted by the competent ecclesiastical authority that, within the limits set for them in the name of the Church, they fulfill a proper function entrusted to them in view of the common good, in accord with the prescripts of law; other juridic persons are private. §2. Public juridic persons are given this personality either through the law itself or by a special decree of the competent authority granting it; private juridic persons are given this personality only through a special decree of the competent authority expressly granting this personality."

Munus or Function

We have already seen that the etymology of the word *munus* is the same as the words *communio* and *ministry*. *Munus* is sometimes rendered in translation as "function" or "purpose" or even "ministry." Vatican II's Decree on the Apostolate of the Laity *Apostolicam actuositatem* recognizes in its sections 23 through 27 certain levels of relationship between the lay apostolate and the hierarchy of the Church:[17]

- some are "praised or recommended by the hierarchy";
- some are "given explicit recognition by the hierarchy";
- for some the hierarchy assumes "a special responsibility";
- others are joined by the hierarchy "more closely with its own apostolic function";
- for some apostolates "the hierarchy entrusts to the laity some functions which are more closely connected with pastoral duties."

Clearly, amidst this hierarchy of apostolic organizations, the Council envisioned that some apostolic activity would be so bound to the mission of the Church that conferral or entrustment of a *munus* would be necessary to authorize its conduct by an organization, "such as the teaching of Christian doctrine, certain liturgical actions, and the care of souls."[18] The text of the above-cited paragraph uses both the words *munia* and *missio* to describe the relationship to ecclesiastical hierarchy, *munia* being synonymous with *munus* and translated variously as *ministry, duty, or function*. The Council thus equates the conferral of a *munus* with a *missio* or commissioning, a sending forth for particular service or duty. Some types of apostolic activity involve a *munus*, and there is a necessary act of commissioning or *missio* by the hierarchy of the Church required for its beginning.

The first distinction, then, between a *public* and a *private* juridic person is the conferral of a *munus*, or the mandate for mission or *missio* given by ecclesiastical authority to a juridic person. The act of *missio* or mandating a certain mission for a public juridic person is an act of *communio* as well: it confers upon an organization or corporate entity a specific *munus* to fulfill in organic unity with the larger Church, and in hierarchic unity with the public authority of the Church. The act of *missio* is the handing over or entrusting of a *munus* or

[17] Vatican II, decree, *Apostolicam actuositatem, 24,* November 18, 1965, *AAS* 58(1966), 837-864.
[18] *Ibid.*

mission, an act of empowerment by the larger Church, to a public juridic person. It is fitting that many Catholic institutions, whether in healthcare or higher education or another apostolic activity, have adopted the role of a senior administrator or executive for mission and ministry, as a function of sponsorship and a guarantor of the fulfillment of the *munus* which the juridic person was commissioned to perform within the Church. Such a person serves as sentry, navigator, and conscience for the institution in fulfillment of its *missio* — that which it was commissioned to do.

Action "In the Name of the Church"

The second distinction is that, for a public juridic person, this *munus* or function is to be carried out "in the name of the Church" (*nomine Ecclesiae*) and not in the name of the juridic person alone. To act in the name of another is to act in relationship to that other. To act in the name of another carries the implication that such action is done with the knowledge and consent of the other. Action by a member of the Christian faithful or group of the Christian faithful "in the name of the Church" is different, however, from action by one physical person in the name of another physical person. Action by a member of the Church "in the name of the Church" is not action on behalf of a second person, a different person, another person — instead, it is action by one person or group in the name of an entire community or *communio fidelium* of which that person or group is a constitutive part.

The point at which individual or group initiative rises to the level of action "in the name of the Church" or the entire community is not entirely certain. Some activities, such as liturgical prayer, are so intimately connected with the life of the community of faith that they are always and everywhere undertaken "in the name of the Church," no matter the actor and no matter the audience. Other activities may be so broad in scope that they bear a relationship to the entire community. In other circumstances it may be the identity of the actor who — by virtue of a relationship to the community of believers — acts "in the name of the Church" (this relationship is often expressed by *jurisdiction* in the Church, such that one who acts with *jurisdiction* acts in *the name of the Church*).

Clearly, then, action "in the name of the Church" is also essentially related to the notion of ecclesial *communio*. Action undertaken in the name of the Church may have the ability — by its nature, by its scope, by virtue of the person acting in relationship to the community, either to enhance and fortify the *communio* of the Church, or to disturb it, even gravely.

Action "in the name of the Church" cannot therefore be undertaken at the private initiative of just any member of the Christian faithful. It demands that it be commissioned by one in a proper relationship to the community of faith: it requires the assent of one with jurisdiction to extend this *missio* in the name of the community. This *missio* is juridically expressed in the conferral of a *munus* or function to act "in the name of the Church."

Action "in the name of the Church" is not identical to action in the name of the hierarchy, even though an action of the hierarchy is necessary to confer the *munus* of a public juridic person. It is not action "in the name of the hierarchy," but rather action "in the name of the Church" as *commissioned* by the hierarchy through the act of *missio* or sending forth. By this act, the work of a public juridic person is joined organically with the larger Church through the bond of *communio* and is joined with the mission of the entire Church to be leaven in the world, servant, herald, teacher, evangelist.

Summary: Private and Public

In sum, what distinguishes a public juridic person from a private juridic person is two-fold: the commission to perform a particular function or *munus*, and the *missio* to do so in the name of the Church. These theological distinctions carry with them certain practical consequences as well.

For the public juridic person, because it bears the burden of carrying out a mission or function in the name of the Church, a greater sense of accountability arises than with a private juridic person, which acts in its own name. Property of a public juridic person becomes "ecclesiastical goods," that is, property considered to be held for the purposes of the Church and administered by the public juridic person. As such, the public juridic person is generally held to observe the fiscal controls and requirements outlined in Book V of the *Code of Canon Law* concerning temporal goods. For a private juridic person, on the other hand, fiscal procedures and requirements should be specified in its statutes and by-laws.

Establishment of a Juridic Person

Who is the ecclesiastical authority competent to establish a juridic person, particularly to confer the *munus* to be entrusted to a public juridic person? The *Code of Canon Law* is not clear about this, but practice has provided some helpful experience. It depends in large measure on the geographic scope of the institution or group.

For juridic persons within a single diocese, the diocesan bishop is certainly competent to issue the decree required for the establishment of a juridic person. For juridic persons with assets or activity in multiple dioceses within the same conference of bishops, the episcopal conference may approve the establishment of the juridic person. In the United States, however, the United States Conference of Catholic Bishops has declined to do so, preferring that multi-diocesan apostolic works be approved by a competent dicastery or congregation of the Holy See. In the sponsorship relationship, many such apostolic works will involve one or more religious institutes, and hence it is the Holy See's Congregation for Institutes of Consecrated Life and Societies of Apostolic Life which is competent to review the statutes of a proposed juridic person and issue a decree establishing it. A Catholic institution of higher education, or consortium of institutions seeking to collaborate in establishing a juridic person for Catholic education, may instead petition the Congregation for Catholic Education for approval and establishment.

Supporting Notions

Sponsorship describes an intent to seek and to define a formal relationship between one entity or group and another, but the term is conceptual and imprecise in itself: it does not define the relationship with precision. Sponsorship as a term is inclusive of multiple discrete realities, each of which demands that choices be made and provisions drafted in legal language. In considering whether the canonical institution of a juridic person is the best vehicle for conveying the desired goals of sponsorship, a set of related ideas should be considered:

- ownership and governance;
- collaboration and accountability toward fulfillment of the mission;
- reasons and motives for sponsorship decisions.

Ownership and Governance

The term historically adopted in canon law for ownership is the Latin word *dominium*. Since ownership of goods in the Church is always oriented toward a religious or charitable end, *dominium* in canon law is more properly understood as stewardship rather than the unfettered liberty of ownership for its own sake and without limitation. *Dominium* in the Church also returns us to the notion of *communio*, since the stewardship over assets and property is always related to the larger ends of the Church itself and its mission in the world. No person, physical or juridic, exercises apostolic work entirely alone in the Church. If one exercises a charism, it is for the good of others.

Unfettered ownership of goods and property for its own sake is not envisioned by the *Code of Canon Law* for a juridic person, but instead stewardship, governance, administration toward an end beyond the purposes of the individual persons who comprise or oversee the juridic person. The Church validates ownership by ecclesiastical entities (and has historically fought to defend the right to such ownership) exclusively so that the goods and property so possessed may be directed toward the charitable and spiritual goals and actions of the Church in the world. Governance of the goods of the Church must be directed exclusively to the religious and charitable ends of the Church. An understanding of this is important not only to the drafting of statutes and bylaws for a juridic person, but for its actual governance, management, and operation. Trustees, officers, directors, administrators and all who are involved in overseeing the work of a juridic person should be thoroughly imbued with the distinctions between ownership and control on one hand, and stewardship and governance toward a spiritual or religious mission on the other.

Governance in the context of sponsorship may be distinct from property ownership or control of assets. In this context governance may be understood not as a static concept involving complete control, but instead as a continuum of control, with some degree of influence as its end or purpose. Governance may be distinct from property ownership. The provisions of canon law do not envision this, but likewise do not prevent it. The canon law structures chosen to exercise governance to one degree or another over the apostolic work of an institution or apostolate need not include canonical ownership of all the goods and property of that institution; *dominium* may be exercised by influencing the decisions, the governance and accountability structures, and the operation of the juridic person, without actually incorporating legal title to property within an ecclesiastical juridic person. This may be a means of ensuring the Catholic identity and operation of an institution without encumbering the juridic person with issues of property administration or exposing it to legal liabilities concomitant with property ownership.

Collaboration and Accountability toward Fulfillment of the Mission

Sponsorship denotes a commitment to collaboration. The very word announces the desire for collaboration between one set of persons and another, or between one institution and another. Collaboration need not be expressed as direct control or governance of the apostolic work, however. Collaboration, just as governance, may be seen as a continuum of discrete choices and options, all of which include levels and mechanisms of accountability for the mission to be undertaken and performed.

For a diocese or religious institute which seeks to remove itself from the immediate governance or administration of an apostolic work or institution, defining sponsorship under the rubric of a juridic person provides the opportunity for broad collaboration with persons and groups other than the religious institute or diocese. Depending on how the juridic person is defined, lay persons (persons other than members of the religious institute or other than clergy or employees of the diocese) may be constituted as members, trustees, directors, officers, members of the finance council of the juridic person, or in a variety of other positions both advisory and deliberative.

Mechanisms of accountability to mission may be expressed in the statutes or operation of the juridic person in a variety of ways. Consider the following options (not exhaustive) as constituting part of the continuum of options for providing an assurance of an orientation toward mission, in an ascending order of participation by the sponsoring religious institute or diocese:

- Prior definition of policy, or rule-making, which defines controls, limits discretionary powers, structures decision-making processes, and defines parameters of action or autonomy. This option paints in broad strokes, as it were, and provides for accountability rather than control.
- Defined and mandated periodic reviews of administrative actions and decisions, or mandatory dispute resolution processes, or defined provisions for audits of administrative and fiscal activity. This option narrows the focus more strictly than the first choice, and provides more targeted mechanisms of accountability.
- Participation in the governance of the juridic person. This may be by guaranteeing a presence of the sponsoring religious institute among the

organization's administrative officers, or among the trustees or directors or finance council. This is often augmented in practice by mandating a senior administrator for mission effectiveness.

- Direct involvement in the discrete actions and decisions of administering the juridic person, through members of the institute as senior administers of the juridic person or through mechanisms of mandatory review and consent for decisions and actions.

Traditionally, the expression of influence over the administration of a sponsored apostolic work has been expressed as "reserved powers" incorporated in the drafting of the work's statutes and bylaws. As this notion of reserved powers has evolved in practice, the nexus between sponsoring religious institute (or diocese) and sponsored apostolic work is seen in three broad areas:

- Explicit approval of corporate documents (statutes, bylaws, and operating procedures);
- Direct appointment or approval of persons in administrative or governance positions (such as CEO, board members, trustees, or officer for mission and ministry);
- Review and consent for certain acts involving property (acquisition or alienation of real property, expenditures involving large sums of money, incurring indebtedness, bond issues).

In sum, the provisions for collaboration and the involvement of persons other than members of the sponsoring religious institute are as broad as the legal imagination of those who draft the statutes and provisions of the juridic person. Opportunities for collaboration with members of the larger community are abundant, but in tandem with mechanisms of collaboration there should also be defined mechanisms for assuring adherence to mission and accountability to sponsor, donors, collaborators, and beneficiaries of services. Both sets of mechanisms, collaboration and accountability, can increase the relative autonomy and quality of service provided by the sponsored institution, along with community involvement, as well as confidence in its Catholic identity and adherence to mission.

Reasons and Motives for Sponsorship Decisions

Dominium in canon law historically has been connected with ownership of property and assets to provide for the institution's mission, not, as was seen above, with ownership for the sake of enrichment or with the liberty of unfettered administration of property. The *dominium* of assets necessary to continue the explicit religious, spiritual, and charitable ends of a canonical entity is described in canon law as the stable patrimony of the juridic person. With the erosion of the doctrine of charitable immunity at civil law in the United States, and a greatly increased tendency to turn to civil courts for relief and remedy against institutions of all kinds and agents of institutions, what were historically considered assets of a diocese, or of a religious institute or a province of the institute, may perhaps be considered liabilities today. This reality may suggest, in particular situations, the segregation of assets and property, to distance a diocese or religious institute from the ownership and control of an apostolic work, or to insulate it and its members from exposure to legal liability. These motives may contribute to certain decisions in the establishment of juridic persons.

The historical roots of *sponsorship* in Roman Law denote an exclusively financial connection; *sponsio* indicated the act of one person serving as financial guarantor or surety for another. In contemporary understanding, however, the term *sponsorship* denotes a different but equivalent relationship, namely the act of serving as guarantor or surety for Catholic identity and mission. Financial ownership, control, and governance may or may not be included in the contemporary religious notion of sponsorship of an institution or apostolic work.

The establishment of a juridic person, or of several juridic persons, may closely parallel civil legal structures such as corporations or trusts, or for the reasons stated above (and others) the canon law juridical structures may be aligned quite differently from the civil structures. Close alignment between structures of law under both legal systems reinforces the legal consequences under both laws: it demonstrates the clear intent to accomplish legally in every way possible the segregation of assets or corporate distinctions and connections desired by the sponsor. A divergence may reveal instead the desire to exercise a different manner of sponsorship, or a different level of *dominium* over the assets and property of the apostolic work, rather than a close parallel with civil legal structures. The motivation for choosing civil structures (often, tax and liability consequences) may be quite different from those for choosing canonical structures (often, assurance of Catholic identity and mission).

It may be preferable that title to real property or to assets which may be exposed to legal attack be held by a civil corporation and not by either the sponsoring religious institute or diocese or the juridic person established to define the sponsorship relationship. If the property was originally held by the diocese, by the religious institute or an apostolic work of that institute, however, the canons on alienation of property must be observed in transferring ownership to a civil corporation. This preference will express itself in the drafting of statutes for the juridic person, since governance and accountability structures will not focus on property ownership and control, but rather on mission and ministry in corporate administration and delivery of services.

It may be preferable to incorporate only a part of the institution or apostolic work, rather than the entire endeavor, as a juridic person at canon law. Alternatively, it may be preferred to establish several juridic persons, each exercising sponsorship or *dominium* or governance over only a component part of the entire apostolic work and its property. Perhaps, in an ecclesiastical twist on a secular legal theme, several dioceses, religious institutes, or other ecclesiastical entities would choose to collaborate in establishing a juridic person to oversee, to administer, or even to own, property and assets for a common purpose. Lastly, one or more sponsoring institutes or dioceses or ecclesiastical entities may choose to form an ecclesiastical "holding company," a juridic person established to hold and administer other subsidiary or component juridic persons, or civil corporations or trusts related to a common mission. Mechanisms for exerting influence and expressing sponsorship for the several works or entities subsidiary to the "holding company" could thus be concentrated and not dissipated among multiple legal realities; duplication of energies and efforts could be minimized. These options should be considered also when forming collaborative or joint ventures with institutions that are not Catholic in their founding or identity, since it is not necessary in canon law (but may be defined in the statutes of the juridic person itself) that all members of the juridic person, or of its administrative officers or bodies, be Catholics in full communion with the Church.

The Church is a Government not a Corporation

At the heart of any decision regarding a relationship or parallel between canon law structures and civil law structures should be this consideration: models of ownership and governance within the Church follow a *governmental* model and not a *corporate* model. The relationship between, for instance, a diocese and a parish (both public juridic persons) is not that of home office and branch office; rather, it is akin to that of state government and local municipal government. Power, ownership, and accountability are all defined in canon law with this understanding. At the core of canonical provisions for ownership and administration is the governance of mission for *communio*, not a corporate hierarchy of ownership and subsidiary branches. Similarly, choices in canonical sponsorship, especially for public juridic persons, should be considered along the model of governmental relationships rather than corporate ownership and control.

For various reasons, not least among them a reluctance or a lack of expertise in explaining our own structures at canon law, their historical development, and the purposes behind them, our North American practice has been to allow civil attorneys to define the Church through the use of the secular corporate models of the civil law. This has not always served the Church well or led to greatest benefit for our apostolic works and ministries. Secular corporate models, even when couched in the language of state charitable and religious corporation statutes, emphasize ownership and control, in contradistinction to the Church's self-understanding of *dominium* and sponsorship, which emphasize collaboration toward mission and toward fulfillment of the spiritual ends of the Church. In canon law, ownership, power, and control cede their secular place of primacy to greater principles such as *communio*, subsidiarity, collaboration, and mission.

A bit more should be said about defining the Church as government and not as corporation. It is for this reason, perhaps among others, that the universal law of the Church erects each parish, each religious institute and province thereof, and other ecclesiastical entities, as public juridic persons in their own right. Ownership and control are not to be objects of controversy in defining structures so important to the delivery of the Church's mission. Each has its own proper administrator, who is not an employee, a servant, or in most instances even an agent of the next "higher" administrator, be it bishop or major superior. The powers of a bishop toward a parish are circumscribed narrowly by the universal law of the Church, and even though he may tax the income of that parish and other juridic (and even private) persons within the diocese, the bishop may not seize or otherwise directly control parish assets or their administration unless through a process of law for grave malfeasance of the administrator. Rather, just as a state may tax persons and corporations within it, the state may not seize or exert direct control over corporate or personal assets except through a process of law related to unlawful activity. Just as a bishop may erect a parish and thereafter receive reports regarding its activities and temporal administration, so a state government may charter a municipality and thereafter receive reports on its activity and administration.

"Inferior" entities within the Church do not relate to hierarchical superiors in a manner consistent with corporate reality, even in most not-for-profit or charitable religious corporations. They do not relate to hierarchical superiors in a manner consistent even with most other religious bodies. The relationship finds its best analog in models of municipal government, and how the actions and entities of municipal government relate to the hierarchically superior state or provincial government. It is not a relationship of ownership and control, but of a (usually) shared vision and set of actions toward the common goal of fostering and protecting the citizens and commerce of the governed territory. Is this not the action of the Church as well, instead of the control of corporate structures?

Decisions of sponsorship relationships and their definition under both canon law and the prevailing civil law must consider carefully how the governance of ministry is reflected, and consider as well that decisions and enactments which may have seemed clear and may have been beneficial in earlier times and climes may now clamor for redefinition or greater precision in mirroring the government of the Church toward spiritual ends.

Indicators for Selecting Public or Private Juridic Personality

The practitioner of canon law cannot devalue or marginalize canonical corporate structures. Although in certain encounters with the secular law canon law defers to its sister science, the theological values which undergird corporate ministry in the Church are far too important to omit in the canonization of structures for ecclesial society. Having said this, what indicators exist to guide a choice of canonical structures? Among them are these: the origin, the means, and the ends of the apostolic work or institution. First, a challenge is presented.

Path Dependence

Considerable attention is being given today in American secular law, as it concerns corporate, governmental, and economic structures and operations, to the theory of "path dependence." We read a definition in a legal commentary by one contemporary author, "Modern corporate governance analyses often invoke path dependence dynamics — the tendency of corporate governance systems to preserve conditions that existed in the past due to economic or political reasons or simply due to historical accident."[19] Path dependence arises

[19] A.N. Licht, "The Mother of All Path Dependencies: Toward a Cross-Cultural Theory of Corporate Governance Systems," *Delaware Journal of Corporate Law* 26(2001)149.

from two sources: it is driven either by the persistence of structures or the persistence of laws. Path dependence leads to "institutional persistence," the continuance of legal, cultural, economic, and corporate structures over time, even after the conditions have changed which gave rise to those institutions. In its extreme, path dependence evolves into rigid structures, inflexible and unyielding in the midst of changing surroundings and the erosion of the supporting infrastructure of values and aspirations.

As institutes within the Church consider new sponsorship models or re-evaluate existing sponsorship relationships, a prayer accompanying the rational legal determinations ought to be for the wisdom and insight to avoid path dependence or an uncritical adherence to past structures and relationships. Legal, institutional, and charismatic inertia ought to be avoided within the Church, lest mission be stifled and confined or its quality and efficiency be compromised out of a fear of change or a lack of creativity in defining structures.

Many dioceses and religious institutes struggle today with the question of maintenance versus mission: are our best energies and resources expended on maintaining structures and institutions, as well as models of service and ministry, which have long existed, or are they best spent on newer, perhaps riskier or less-defined, models of ministry and service?

Origin of the Apostolic Work

Upon some entities is conferred a juridic status by law. We have already enumerated some of those which are created public juridic persons *de iure*. When something is created a juridic person by an action of the law itself, that is, by indirect provision of the supreme legislator, the result is always a public juridic person.

Competent ecclesiastical authority may also validly issue a decree erecting a juridic person, but the result will not be automatic: the decree of erection must state whether the entity is constituted *public* or *private*.[20] The origin or founding of an entity is not therefore an absolute indicator of its proper status, but only one part of the intermix of criteria.

A religious institute today is normally not founded quickly, but instead follows a certain developmental trajectory. Perhaps starting life as a private association of the faithful, a group of individuals enter into association to pursue a common charism and common life. Growth in members may bring the resultant movement along the trajectory to private juridic person, and continued

[20] Except, of course, the erection of a public association of the faithful as a juridic person, which always designates public juridic personality.

time and vocations may lead the group to seek and achieve public juridic status, even of pontifical right.

These examples, few among many which could be crafted, merely caution that the initial founding of an organization or associative apostolate does not attach it to a particular juridical category. Origin is but one part of the larger complex of indicators which will determine proper status in the current law.

If an apostolic work, such as a hospital, nursing home, or health care system, or perhaps an institution of higher education, was founded by a religious institute, itself a public juridic person, it may be proper to consider that the sponsored apostolic work should continue as a new public juridic person. A diocesan social service system, cemetery, retreat center, or other ministry may have been founded as part of the diocese itself, but it may be proper now to consider a different sponsorship model, perhaps its own juridic person.

Individuals may approach an ecclesiastical superior, whether diocesan bishop or religious major superior, with a dream, a vision, a goal, a promise, a hope or even a realistic plan for a new venture into ministry, or with a gift to endow such a ministry. It may be proper to consider the origin of that new venture as one among the criteria for selecting the most appropriate structure under both laws for the governance of its operation: canonically, perhaps an association of the faithful, a private juridic person, or a public juridic person.

Rules on administration and alienation of property will be defined in broad strokes by law (Book V of the *Code of Canon Law*) and further specified by the particular law of the juridic person's statutes and bylaws. Catholic identity may be assured by mechanisms defined in statutes. Accountability is provided for, again at least in broad strokes, by the Code, and further defined in particular or proper law as well as statutes. Origin, or how the sponsored work came into being, may be one of the criteria for making legal choices.

Means: The Operation of the Apostolic Organization

Another indicator is the means employed by an entity to accomplish its goals. Diverse activities determine its means of acting, including a) how an entity finances its works; b) the amount and scope of its monetary or temporal holdings; c) the geographic range of its operations and works; d) its self-portrayal as "Catholic" or not; e) the closeness or identification of its work and ministries to the public authority of the Church; f) the possibility that a work may expose one or more church-related institutions to liability or injurious judgments, even in the secular Courts;[21] g) the relationship of its administrator(s) or trustee(s) with the larger or public Church;[22] and, lastly, h) the particular business form or corporate structure adopted in the secular law, along with its concomitant obligations, ought to be considered when assessing how it affects the relationship of the undertaking with the larger Church and with secular society.

Ends: The Nature of the Apostolic Activity

Certain apostolic activities arise from the heart of the Church itself or are so closely allied with the central mission of the Church that their conduct demands close attention. There are some ministries which must, of their essence, be conducted "in the name of the Church." The Vatican II decree on the apostolate of the laity *Apostolicam actuositatem*[23] identified some of these apostolic activities as including promotion of public worship and the teaching of Catholic doctrine. Their closeness to the Church is protected by the canons, which proscribe their undertaking without ecclesiastical origin or approbation.

Because of the perception that such endeavors cannot be undertaken apart from the Church but only by the Church or in the name of the Church, they must of necessity be conducted only by public juridic persons or their equivalent. This establishes one set of objective criteria for determining the canonical status of an apostolic work: for these ministries, the choice of corporate form is no longer subjective. They demand the reciprocal accountability and the legal concomitants afforded by public juridic personality.

[21] Canon 1295 mandates enhanced fiscal controls for any fiscal transaction which might worsen the patrimonial condition of a public juridic person. Enhanced exposure to liability resulting from a transaction is an example. In assessing the appropriateness of a particular juridical form for an apostolic undertaking, one might include this issue in the decision-making process.

[22] Public scrutiny will notice critically the activities of, for instance, several prominent bishops, archbishops, or cardinals among the directors or trustees of a church-related institution, perhaps itself suggesting the adoption of a juridic category with more rigorous standards for fund-raising and fiscal management. *Jurisdiction* in the Church is in part an expression of *relationship* between the actor and the community acted upon. The extent or scope of relationship between an officer or public representative of the organization and the larger community of faith ought perhaps then to be a criterion (though by no means the sole or principal criterion) for assessing the propriety of a given juridic status.

[23] Vatican II, decree, *Apostolicam actuositatem*, November 18, 1965; *AAS* 58 (1966), 837-864.

SUMMARY

Various factors motivate the desire of a religious institute to specify its sponsorship role of an apostolic work or institution. For many such works, the appropriate form for specifying the relationship is that of a separate *public juridic person*. Although itself lacking precision in meaning, the notion of sponsorship can impel a religious institute to seek legally-precise means of defining structures of relationship, which in sponsorship will often involve an influence, but not control, over the operations and mission of a sponsored activity or institution. The statutes of the juridic person provide the means for defining the structures and mechanisms of influence, principally through structures of collaboration and accountability. Within the Church, legal constructs and institutes such as the public juridic person exist not to define lines of ownership and supervision, as in civil corporate models, but rather participation and accountability in mission, which is more akin to government in secular society. Undergirding all of the structures for collaboration, participation, accountability, and responsibility is the desire to foster and maintain *communio* within the Church among all persons and apostolic endeavors. In so doing, all citizens of the City of God cooperate in its building up and all witness the grace of God in the charisms freely exercised for the good of all.

CHAPTER FIVE

The Sponsorship Relationship: Incorporation and Dissolution Civil and Canon Law Perspectives

PATRICIA M. DUGAN, ESQ.

Introduction

The pathways into and out of sponsorship relationships can be as numerous as the reasons and goals that initiate sponsorship of a ministry[1] in the first place. This paper will trace the most basic concepts and statutes, canonical and civil, which form the sponsorship relationship from a legal point of view.

Whenever a lawyer begins a relationship with a client, the first task is to establish the goal. What is it the client wants this lawyer to accomplish? If the answer is to establish a Catholic sponsorship relationship, there are two areas of law that must both be followed: canon law and civil law.

Civil law contains numerous specialties: federal and state law, criminal, corporate, tax, family, employment and securities, among other concentrations. But once an attorney finds the niche law to fit the case's fact situation, there are also the questions of what the federal law says about an issue and what a state's law says about an issue. Federal law covers anything that occurs within the United States, is covered specifically by federal statute, and/or involves a United States constitutional question. State law covers everything that occurs in a specific state, and is covered by state law only. For instance, a tax lawyer must know the federal tax code as well as the tax code of the state in which the client functions. The same is true with every concentration or type of law. Either the federal law or the state law will be the controlling law on an issue,

[1] By ministry is meant continuing the mission of the church both in the name of, and on behalf of, the faith community.

and that will dictate which court has jurisdiction,[2] or actually handles any litigation in a case, and what law is applied.

In matters involving sponsorship, the most applicable civil laws are corporate, tax, employment, real property, and contract law. Corporate law involves the laws of the state where the corporation is formed and registered, as well as those in any state in which the corporation is doing business. Tax laws are predominantly federal laws, especially when those which determine whether or not a corporation is a profit or non-profit corporation for purposes of paying taxes and raising funds.[3] Employment, real property and contract law will involve the law of the state in which the corporation operates. Regulations, such as those that govern medical records and patient or student rights, and anti-trust activities are most often federal based.

Canon Law is first and foremost *universal law*.[4] A credentialed canon lawyer can, generally speaking, practice canon law anywhere in the world.[5] Universal law is also sometimes referred to as common law which is the law that is found in the Code of Canon Law and in subsequent, universal, legal texts. Canon law also provides for *particular law*[6] which applies to a territory like a diocese, or the territory included in a nation's conference of bishops.[7] Finally, canon law also includes *proper law* which relates to religious institutes and their members. Proper law is usually found specifically in the constitutions and rules of the various religious institutes who frequently are the sponsors in the sponsorship relationship.

[2] In civil law jurisdiction is the legal concept of determining which court is the appropriate or legally correct court to have the power, right, or authority to interpret and apply its law to a legal controversy or litigation.

[3] Non-profit corporations are permitted to profit for the corporation, but not for individuals. Both profit and non-profit corporations may earn a profit, the difference is what each can do with their net earnings and still maintain the non-profit status.

[4] See CIC 1983, c. 12 § 1: Universal laws bind everywhere all those for whom they were issued.

[5] A canon lawyer is someone who has studied in an accredited canon law faculty and passed the license examination. Not all licensed canon lawyers can perform all canon law functions as outlined in the code. For instance, a canon lawyer cannot serve as a Judicial Vicar unless he is a cleric (c. 1420). To serve as a judge, a canon lawyer who is a lay person must be specially permitted by the conference of Bishops, and serve only within the context of a collegial judicial panel (c. 1421).

[6] CIC 1983, Canon 12, § 3: Laws established for a particular territory bind those for whom they were issued as well as those who have a domicile or quasi-domicile there, and who, at the same time, are actually residing there.

[7] An example of particular law can be seen in the holy days of obligation. Not all religious feast days are holy days in all places. The Conference of Bishops determines the holy days of obligation for its particular territory.

These three types of canon law frequently overlap, especially when establishing sponsorship relationships. Application of these laws may vary from place to place, just as civil laws vary from state to state.[8] Time is also a factor in how any law is interpreted. What was of utmost importance in one decade can be of almost no significance in the next decade, especially as it pertains to the subject of sponsorship. When the present *Code of Canon Law* was promulgated in 1983, there was a rush to specifically interpret the nuts and bolts issues of church property, responsibility and liability. Issues such as alienation of property and mergers of property have now been superseded by issues of mission and identity.

Pathways into Sponsorship: Civil Law

The most useful and usual pathway into a sponsoring relationship is the formation of a corporation. This legal structure was developed in England toward the end of the thirteenth century, when the law first recognized this corporate legal personality in addition to the individual legal personality of citizens. A business could form a legal personality unto itself, separate and apart from the original, individual owner. Laws gradually developed governing these corporations and protecting them, all as a way to encourage the development of business in the town.

Today, as then, assets and liabilities can be placed into a corporation. In this way the assets and liabilities of the individual could be protected in the event the business was not successful. Legislatures and courts allowed them to be placed behind a "corporate veil", separate from the individual owner. If the business were to become bankrupt with outstanding debts, these debts could only be satisfied to the total of the corporate assets. A corporate officer could not be forced to pay corporate debts by selling or mortgaging his own home. Corporations were allowed to exercise recognized corporate powers and rights as provided by the law, and by their articles of incorporation and bylaws.

Catholic institutions, especially health care, higher education, and social service, are turning to new sponsorship relationships both to survive in operation and to carry on the mission in the name of the Church. The majority of

[8] The overlap of canon and civil law raises the newest issues confronting the sponsorship relationship. Canon 22 outlines a process known as the "canonization of civil law". For some issues canon law does not provide its own norms but defers to the local civil law. Whenever this happens, the civil law must be observed and as such, will have the same effect as if it were specific canon law. When civil law directly conflicts with specific norms in canon law, canon law must prevail and an ecclesiastical judge or superior of a religious institute must work to enforce the canon law first and foremost.

these Catholic institutions are incorporated civilly and separately, standing as civil legal entities, distinct from their sponsoring religious or Church communities or dioceses. Their governance is accomplished through independent boards of trustees which also often include non-Catholic members. Their staff and personnel also frequently include non-Catholics who may also serve in leadership roles. Usually the recipients of their work are not just members of the faith community, but the public at large. And in considering this evolution of sponsorship roles, it is important to note that usually Catholic institutions receive little funding from the religious sponsor or for that matter, any Church source. They may accept government financing and aid and conform to government and First Amendment requirements to receive that aid.

Sponsorship is neither a legal nor a technical term. It can be a way for religious institutes, facing declining membership, to continue to insure their Catholic work. The use of the civil law structure of incorporation allows the religious institute to use corporate reserved powers in order to maintain its Catholic influence on the works performed by the sponsored entity. These reserved powers, enumerated in the articles of incorporation and corporate bylaws, can include the appointment of members of the board of directors or trustees, establishing and amending the corporate purpose and mission, setting the rules for merging, selling or dissolving the corporate entity; approving the annual budget; appointing the chief executive officer; and amendment of the articles of incorporation and the corporate bylaws themselves.

The grayest area between the civil and canon law systems is that of ownership. Questions of ownership in these matters can be extremely complicated. They necessitate an initial and ongoing comprehensive and complete inventory of goods to be placed in the sponsored entity or to be entrusted to the sponsoring entity. Ownership can become the Achilles heel for the Church sponsor. The Church does not, even through the religious sponsor, have any real ownership with regard to the institution or its works.

Any goods owned by a public juridic person[9] are ecclesiastical goods. It is crucial to the success of the sponsorship relationship to define precisely whether from civil law perspective a given sponsor owns its institution or works, or whether the sponsor is only the administrator of the works Ownership questions can rapidly become issues of mistrust and misunderstanding among the

[9] Public juridic persons in the Catholic Church are erected groups of persons or things which carry out their mission in the name of the Church. See canons 113 through 123 for the general norms of canon law addressing juridic personality. The public juridic person is the canon law entity most comparable to the civil law corporation.

participants. By investing time and effort in the initial inventory much negative territorial emotion can be avoided later.

Many Church models, such as joint ownership, exist today, but enough time has not passed to assess their long term rate of success or failure. There are also multiple forms of acquiring ownership through transactions such as merger, consolidation, asset acquisition, holding company, or joint operating company. Whether or not any one of these is a possibility for a sponsor to use is dependent in part on the state laws governing the sponsor and its activities.

Both civil law corporations and sponsorship models begin with statements of purpose, which sometimes encompass goals. This is extremely important for any entity seeking recognition at civil law as a non-profit organization. Many groups, especially those operating within a diocese, may operate under the one umbrella of the diocesan entity, even using the diocesan tax exemption for their multiple endeavors. Under new models of sponsorship this umbrella approach, either with a diocese or religious institute, is neither practical nor desired. Once the purpose or mission statement is clarified in writing, the corporate structure must be addressed: board members and officers must be identified; duties drawn up and memorialized; terms of office, succession processes, and other particulars addressed. Apostolic works once directly controlled by leaders of religious institutes have morphed into multi-tiered boards with multiple purposes and goals. When drafting articles of incorporation and bylaws for these complex entities, it is equally important to address tax and antitrust law and regulations which change with some regularity.

From the perspective of Catholic identity, the Catholic institution and its sponsor must make certain that any essential and non-negotiable characteristics of Catholic identity are precisely enunciated in the legal documents of corporate formation. This is to insure that Catholic identity is maintained and influences the delivery of services for which the ministry was established in the first place. Canon law does not supply a list of Catholic values to include in legal documents. Instead these are generally accepted principles which should be tailored to the particular work of the corporation. Catholic tradition has always leaned heavily on organized structures, especially its apostolic institutions and religious institutes, as the most effective manner in which to continue its mission to educate, care for the sick and serve the poor. These institutions and the evolving models of sponsorship are good not only for the Church but for society as a whole.

Catholic institutions, their assets, and their functions, exist for the sole purpose of accomplishing the mission of Jesus as understood in the teachings, values and tradition of the Catholic Church. These institutions, through their sponsors, maintain some type of communion with Catholic Church authority. Many models of participation in the ministry of the Church have existed and are evolving for the purpose of accomplishing the mission of Jesus. The most frequently used models include: direct sponsorship by the religious institute or diocese, the public juridic person, and the association of Christian faithful.

Canon law, due in part to its universal nature, was not designed to deal with some of the contemporary issues sponsorship faces today in the United States. While the 1983 *Code of Canon Law* includes a section on the teaching office of the Church and its educational institutions, there is no reference to Catholic healthcare facilities at all. The code did not envision multi-congregational or multi-diocesan ownership of apostolic works, which characterize much of Catholic healthcare in the U.S. today. Such complex structures and joint ventures require great precision of language to ensure clarity of the desired relationship.

The word "trustee" does not appear in the code, but rather uses other designations such as steward, administrator or council member. When dealing with multi-tiered boards, it is important to distinguish who are trustees satisfying corporate civil law requirements, and who is fulfilling canonical requirements. Often a trustee may serve as both, but that is neither a requirement nor a recommendation. Such dual roles depend entirely on the sponsor, the mission, the corporate documents and the activities involved in the ministry.

In Book V, The Temporal Goods of the Church, the *Code of Canon Law* sets out a number of specific duties for anyone who has assumed the administration of ecclesiastical, temporal goods. These include: respecting the intention of the donor;[10] the taking of an oath;[11] preparing a detailed inventory of goods;[12] the observance of civil law and canon law in all transactions;[13] the maintenance of goods with adequate insurance coverage;[14] the observing of civil law in all matters pertaining to personnel such as payment of salaries;[15] the presentation to the faithful of an accounting of the use made of any donations

[10] C. 1267, § 3.
[11] C. 1283, 1°.
[12] C. 1283, 2°.
[13] C. 1284, § 2.
[14] C. 1284, § 2.
[15] C. 1286.

received;[16] the securing of the bishop's permission before initiating or contesting any civil law suits;[17] and, the observance of testamentary clauses when goods are bequeathed to the Church.[18]

As these specific canons exemplify, where there is responsibility in canon law, there is also liability. Here there is a great overlapping of civil and canon law implications. If an act is invalid canonically, even if it is valid civilly, the administrator or trustee who acted, is also liable for the invalidity. Actions such as selling property or incurring major debts without the proper approval, or using funds for purposes other than the intent of the donor, are strictly regulated in canon law, even more so than in civil law. Even though such actions are regulated in canon law, the sponsor in its formulation of the sponsor relationship, should acknowledge that canon law also pertains and make it part of the civil structure.

In addition to the complex issues facing global society today, one reason for the need for new models of sponsoring health care, education and social services by Catholic institutions has been the dearth of vocations to the religious institute. Other issues impacting this are academic freedom, bioethical advances and the rapid pace of scientific, cultural and political changes in the world. After more than a decade, it has become evident that time is needed to develop not only the canonical models but also the supporting structures within those models, such as the training and development of staff and leadership.

Public Juridic Persons

Among the areas of concern regarding emerging sponsorship relationships, the Holy See has expressed concern about the membership of boards, monitoring the application of the ethical and religious boundaries, and compensation to the religious institute upon the transfer of assets to a new entity. Some religious institutes, especially from the English-speaking world, have begun exploring new sponsorship models by asking the Holy See for juridic personality for their developing apostolates. While these institutes still have the religious personnel to manage their work themselves, they have already brought laity and even non-Catholics into their work as collaborators. By seeking separate juridic personality at this early point in the process, the religious institute is able to exert the most influence on the new juridic personality as it develops.

[16] C. 1287, § 2.
[17] C. 1288.
[18] C. 1300.

The first issue the Holy See addresses is competence, or, exactly where such petitions for juridic personality should be decided. Canon law does not stipulate competence for the erection of public juridic personality. The first petition of this kind was sent to the United States Conference of Catholic Bishops to determine competence to grant the public juridic personality. It was eventually determined that ordinarily the ministry of the proposed juridic person would be the determining factor for competence. If the ministry is education, the appropriate dicastery is the Congregation for Catholic Education. If the ministry involves health care currently sponsored by a pontifical religious institute the petition should be directed to Congregation for Institutes of Consecrated Life and Societies of Apostolic Life (CICLSAL). In the situation of a diocesan bishop seeking to establish a diocesan institution as a public juridic person that petition would be addressed to the Congregation for the Clergy, which handles all diocesan alienation of temporal goods.

The nature of the parties to the petition affects how the petition may be viewed by the Holy See. Partnership between a religious institute and a for-profit corporation is usually viewed as a last resort to keep services flowing to those in need of those services. Partnership between a Catholic entity and a non-Catholic, non-profit entity would be more readily granted when the sponsoring religious institute retains at least fifty percent in the sponsorship relationship via impact on the governing board, or some other reserved power.

The CICLSAL also decides requests for permission by religious institutes to sell institutions to secular buyers some of which have agreed to continue them as Catholic entities. Even in the civil world this is not an enforceable option. The sale can be approved and completed, but once it is, there is no reliable way for the Catholic contingency of the agreement to be overseen or carried out. Civil law would become mired in issues of Catholicity and First Amendment claims. The CICLSAL holds the view that once the institution is sold to a non-Catholic buyer, it is no longer under the competency of the CICLSAL, nor under any Church authority. The religious institute proposing such a sale must make sure that the diocesan bishop is informed of the sale and the buyer must be made aware of the concerns of that bishop. Beyond that, once the transfer is concluded it no longer comes under the jurisdiction of the Church.

Once a petition is submitted, the competent Vatican dicastery looks to the defined ministry's identity, purpose and governance structures. As in civil law, the more precisely these are defined, the more easily they are understood in canonical terms as well. Reserved powers must be clear and well defined since these powers are the particular insurers that Catholic identity remains viable and strong in the public juridic person. It is helpful for the petitioner to recognize the importance of the Episcopal Conference in its work, as well as that of the diocesan bishop and local Church. Deference to ethical and moral norms, service to the community of faith, care of individual persons and social justice according to the magisterium of the Church, are all elements which the Holy See looks for when reviewing a petition.[19]

Enough cannot be said about the importance to the Holy See of the reserved powers of the religious institute. These are already defined in the civil articles of incorporation, but must be as precisely and fully defined in the petition for the erection of the public juridic person as is possible. In discussing reserved powers, it would be important to distinguish between powers reserved to the religious institute when the apostolate has simply separate civil incorporation and the powers reserved to the members when the apostolate becomes a new public juridic person, some of whom may be members of the religious institute. The latter, the physical persons who govern the new juridic person, in fact, take over most or all of the powers once reserved to the religious superiors and councils.[20] The Holy See is particularly interested in who has the ability to alter the philosophy or mission of the public juridic person, change the governing statutes, perpetuate the Catholic identity and how, approve the sale of ecclesiastical goods and incur debts to the public juridic person. The Holy See is not interested in the civil law documents of identity for the petitioner, but it is critical to the survival of the public juridic person that the reserved powers in the civil documentation and the petition to the Holy See mirror each other.

Finally, in deciding whether to grant juridic personality, as in other types of alienation, the competent Congregation will seek out the opinions of the bishops of the dioceses in which the institutions are located. This should not be the first time that bishops hear of the petition for approval of the public juridic person. A full open dialogue should have already taken place with the bishops, and all concerns and questions addressed before the petition actually goes to the Holy See.

Some requests for approval by the Holy See have been answered in a timely manner. Other requests have been pending for several years. When there have been questions regarding a particular request these seem to be more concerned with board roles and responsibilities and mission rather than with specific financial issues.

[19] Sharon Holland, I.H.M, "Sponsorship and the Vatican", in *Health Progress* (July – August, 2001) 32-37, 52.
[20] Ibid.

Once approval of the petition for public juridic personality is approved by the Holy See, a relationship begins between the Holy See and the new public juridic person. The Holy See must approve certain acts of alienation of property, especially ones which could endanger the stable patrimony of the juridic person. Holy See approval is also needed to change the statutes or the purpose of the public juridic person.

To maintain its status a public juridic person must comply with any request by the competent Congregation to discuss issues of administration or temporal goods. This, however, does not assign liability to the Holy See for the public juridic person. Canonically, the Holy See has no economic responsibility for the juridic person once approval has been granted. Civil liability has proven elusive due to a myriad of legal entanglements, starting with the question of jurisdiction of a local U.S. court over the Holy See.

Finally, public juridic persons must file annual reports with the competent Congregation. This parallels the obligation of diocesan juridic persons in canon 1287, paragraph 1, referring to the administration of temporal goods. Besides this financial aspect, the juridic person must report on all other relevant matters, including such things as vigilance to its mission and preservation of its Catholic identity. In this report equal emphasis should be given to the development and training of leadership through retreats, conferences and seminars, as much as to progress achieved in growth of the ministry, service delivery, etc.

Pathways Out: Civil Law

Exiting a civil corporate structure is far easier than entering it, but the process still entails certain affirmative actions. The purpose of these actions is to terminate the corporate entity in the same way a death certificate testifies to the death of a person. How a corporation is dissolved is outlined in the corporate law of every state. The dissolution must be voted on by the officers and trustees as outlined in the articles of incorporation and bylaws of the corporation. Because dissolution of the corporation is generally a reserved power of the members, the final decision regarding dissolution remains with the members. In most states the minutes of the members' meeting where the final action is taken must be filed with the state's corporations office. Final tax returns must be filed when the disposition of all corporate property has been accomplished. Those final tax returns, both federal and state, must reflect any income earned in those dispositions. Each state has its own laws on liability and the length of time liability continues. If the corporate name has been trademarked or registered as a trading or doing business name (dba) that must be terminated within the appropriate state or federal registrar. Once the official acts of the corporation have been finished and the corporate assets have been distributed, the pathway out is completed.

Pathways Out: Canon Law

As stated previously, the alienation of property must be approved by the Congregation with competence over the public juridic person. After the request for suppression or extinction of a public juridic person established by the Holy See has gone through the processes required by its own statutes, the matter then passes on to the Holy See for approval. The Holy See has the final approval over the disposition of the patrimony of the public juridic person. If the pathway out is a merger with another entity, the process followed for the initial petition seeking public juridic personality would be submitted to the competent Congregation.

There is also the possibility of a pathway out that is involuntary. In such a situation the competent ecclesiastical authority can suppress the public juridic person. If it is a diocesan public juridic person, it is usually the diocesan bishop who suppresses it. If it is a pontifical juridic person, the competent ecclesiastical authority is the authority which established it. Reasons for suppression of a public juridic person may include: failure to operate according to its statutes, scandal, financial collapse or simply the request of the governing body indicated in the same statutes. The particulars of the process used to suppress the public juridic person may vary from one Vatican congregation to congregation.

Conclusion

Whether the sponsorship relationship is beginning or ending, it is evident that the assistance of both civil and canonical counsel is necessary. Those parties to the sponsorship relationship must make it clear to their counsel – both civil and canonical - exactly what the purpose of the sponsor relationship is and how it to be achieved. If this is done first with the stated goal of perpetually preserving Catholic identity, the structures necessary to carry on the ministry will be achieved and the transition will be seamless.

CHAPTER SIX

SPONSORSHIP IN HIGHER EDUCATION

PAUL L. GOLDEN, CM

INTRODUCTION

In the history of Catholic higher education in the United States, sponsorship is a relatively new term. For more than one hundred and fifty years after the founding of Georgetown University in 1789, the first Catholic institution of higher education in the United States, there was no question that a religious institute[1] or a diocese owned, operated, staffed, managed and shaped the life of the Catholic colleges and universities. Even after many institutions of higher education obtained civil incorporation, the role of the religious institute or diocese remained clear. Today the leaders of these Catholic institutions of higher education and these same religious institutes and dioceses are engaged in a dialogue about sponsorship. This paper will examine how this change came about, what it means canonically, and what change the future may hold.

This paper is limited to Catholic institutions of higher education in the United States, excluding seminaries and specialized schools such as health professional centers. Because there are only fifteen Catholic colleges in the United States not sponsored by religious institutes, this paper will focus on the almost 200 institutions that have traditionally been associated with a religious institute. Much of what follows applies also to the thirteen schools sponsored by arch/dioceses.[2] However because there are sufficient differences in governance, these institutions will not be directly addressed.

[1] When the term "religious institute" is used in this paper, secular institutes and societies of apostolic life are included.

[2] The two Catholic institutions not sponsored by religious institutes or dioceses are Ave Maria College in Ypsilanti, MI and Christendom College in Front Royal, VA.

Sponsorship has no legal meaning in either canon or civil law and therefore has no legal definition. The term *sponsor* comes from the Latin word meaning pledge or promise. So, etymologically, a sponsor is someone who gives assurance. Liturgically, when one sponsors a candidate for Baptism or Confirmation, one gives assurance that the initiate will be properly instructed in the faith and the sponsor pledges to assist in this goal.

Canonists have understood sponsorship as a reservation of civil law control of certain actions to the public juridic person that founded or sustained an incorporated apostolate that canonically remains a part of the public juridic person. This control should be sufficient for the canonical stewards or guarantors to meet their canonical obligations in regard to the activities of the incorporated apostolate.[3]

As religious institutes incorporated their apostolic works, including their colleges and universities, there was a gradual evolution in the language used to describe the religious institute's relationship to these apostolic works. The traditional canonical term *dominium* (ownership) means the limited right of control over goods and property.[4] While the Code of Canon Law does use this term ownership, it more often describes the function as "...acquiring, possessing, administering and alienating goods."[5] Ecclesiastical goods are entrusted to the care of religious institutes for a specific mission. Since the 1970s the word that has been used to best describe the relation between a religious institute and its incorporated work is sponsorship. The meaning of sponsorship, as we will see, continues to evolve. In recent years, those writing about sponsorship have emphasized its elements of mission and *communio*. Moving from owning and controlling, sponsorship now addresses the need to assure that the charism of the founding religious institute is vibrant on campus and that its Catholic identity is lived in an effective manner.

[3] Daniel C. Conlin, "Sponsorship at the Crossroads," *Health Progress* 82 (July- Aug., 2001) 20.

[4] See cc. 635 §1 and 1257 §1.

[5] See cc. 634 §1, 1254 §1 and 1255.

The Classic Model

Before Vatican II, there was a certain similarity in the governance of Catholic colleges. The religious institute, as a public juridic person under canon law, considered these institutions of higher education to be among their apostolate works. The institute often had a great financial and personnel investment in the institution. Many of the colleges and universities carried the name of the institute or its founder or foundress. The religious institute was closely identified with the educational facility and many of its members held top administrative and academic positions. While the large majority of religious institutes had but one college, some had more.[6]

The major superior of the sponsoring institute and his/her council were regularly involved in the administration of the college in numerous ways. The financial health of the school was closely monitored by the religious leadership. The major superior might also have been the president of the school or may have directly appointed the president. The appointment of members of the institute to the faculty and staff was an act of the religious leader. Often there was a long range plan of sending a member of the community away for graduate work in a specific discipline in order that, after completing the degree, the religious would be hired by the school. The canons governing church property were followed. Authorization for such transactions as acquiring or selling property, erecting a building, or undertaking extensive capital improvements were required from the religious institute's leaders.[7] If the local institute's leadership was unable to authorize these transactions on its own, necessary permission was sought from the institute's General Superior and, if necessary, from the appropriate Vatican Congregation. If the local Ordinary had a question or a concern related to the college/university, he might contact either the president of the college or the religious superior.

Before Vatican II, the Catholic colleges and universities in the U.S. were for the most part civilly incorporated. However, the governance of the schools was still closely tied to the religious institute. In 1947 Alcuin Tasch, O.S.B. reported that "...over 90% of Catholic colleges and universities are under the direct

[6] According to the Association of Catholic Colleges and Universities, the Society of Jesus (Jesuits) sponsors 28 institutions, the Institute of the Sisters of Mercy in the Americas , 14 and the Dominican Sisters, 13. (Although drawing from a common heritage the Dominican Sisters are actually separate canonical entities.)

[7] Alice Gallin, *Independence and a New Partnership in Catholic Higher Education* (Notre Dame, IN: University of Notre Dame Press, 1996) 104.

control of some 50 religious orders of men and women."[8] Tasch summarized the various organizational and administrative structures found in more than fifty Catholic colleges and universities surveyed at that time in this way:

> (1) The Religious Corporation is the parent corporation and owns the property and facilities used by the college. (2) There is but one Corporation, the Religious, which conducts the college as one of its activities. (3) The Religious Corporation or community, in all cases, furnishes most of the personnel, administration, and faculty for the college. (4) Religious Superiors constitute the board of trustees, either entirely or in majority ratio. (5) Religious superiors exercise their canonical prerogative of the disposition of their subjects in the matter of appointments. (6) Religious corporations and/or religious superiors exercise certain financial controls below the limits set by Canon Law for the Holy See. (7) The president may also be the religious superior, local or major.[9]

By the early 1960s there was a great deal of pressure from both inside and outside these Catholic institutions to change this kind of governance structure.

Pressures to Change

At the time Vatican II was convoked, American Catholics had reached a new level of prosperity and influence in the country. With a Catholic as president of our country, more Catholics serving in public life and many Catholics as leaders of major corporations, the Catholic colleges and universities felt the need to ensure that their institutions were competitive with their secular counterparts. Catholic leaders called for rigorous academic programs, not only in the humanities but also in the sciences. Institutes of higher learning needed to begin or to further develop their public relations and advancement programs. Processes were needed to ensure academic freedom for faculty appropriate for a Church-related school.

Seeking recognition from the respective accrediting bodies presented its own challenges. One criteria for accreditation was independence and each institution had to demonstrate that it was both financially independent and self governed. As the colleges moved toward being truly American institutions, they also faced the need for resources for both program and capital improvements. In 1963 the U.S. Congress passed the Higher Education Facilities Act

[8] Alcuin W. Tasch, "Organization and Statutes," *College Organization and Administration*, ed. Roy Deferrari (Washington, DC: The Catholic University of America Press, 1947) 62.
[9] Ibid., 47.

(HEFA) that provided funds for campus facilities. A few years later, the Maryland Court of Appeals ruled that the Maryland State construction grants could not be awarded to three church-related schools because they were sectarian.[10] While the decision applied only in the jurisdiction of Maryland, the fact that two of the barred institutions were Catholic captured the attention of all Catholic colleges around the country.

Francis Gallagher, an attorney for one of the colleges affected by the ruling, advised the Catholic higher education community that if colleges and universities wanted to avail themselves of public financial assistance, many changes would have to be initiated. Among his recommendations were expanding lay membership on governing boards, separating the office of college president from that of religious superior and placing the real estate and other property of the college in a separate and independent corporation.[11]

Catholic colleges and universities in the United States worked quickly to change their governance structures so that they were independent of the religious communities who had founded and sponsored them. In the 1971 decision of the Tilton v Richardson case, the four Catholic colleges in Connecticut named in the suit[12] for being in violation of the establishment clause of the U.S. Constitution were found to be not "pervasively sectarian" and therefore eligible for federal funding through the HEFA.[13] The effort to change the structures of the institutions often resulted in their being seen as legally independent and on a par with their non-sectarian peers.

At the same time these changes were underway, the Second Vatican Council in session during 1962-1965, produced several documents which had direct bearing on Catholic higher education, particularly related to lay involvement in this endeavor. In the *Dogmatic Constitution on the Church*[14] an entire chapter was devoted to the laity. Through baptism and confirmation lay men and women share in the mission of the Church (#33) and in the office of Christ as prophet, priest and king. It is the special vocation of the laity to seek the kingdom of God by engaging in temporal affairs and directing them according to

[10] For a fuller discussion of this *Horace Mann* case, see Alice Gallin, *Negotiating Identity: Catholic Higher Education Since 1960* (Notre Dame, IN: University of Notre Dame Press, 2000), 36 and Peter Harrington, "Civil and Canon Law Issues Affecting American Higher Education 1948-1998: An Overview and the ACCU Perspective," *Current Issues in Catholic Higher Education* 20 (Fall, 1999) 51ff.

[11] Harrington, 52.

[12] Sacred Heart University, Fairfield University, Albertus Magnus College and Annhurst College (closed in 1980).

[13] Gallin, *Negotiating Identity*, 37-38.

[14] Vatican II, dogmatic constitution, *Lumen gentium*, November 21, 1964: *AAS* 57 (1965), 5-67.

God's will (#31). Laypersons were encouraged to bring their gifts and talents to assist the Church in accomplishing its mission. The *Pastoral Constitution on the Church in the Modern World*[15] urged the Church and each of its members to devote their energies to the world in which they live and, by doing so, they serve God just as genuinely as by worship. Catholics were encouraged to become more involved in society and in all activities that can further the spreading of the Good News. The *Decree on the Apostolate of the Laity*[16] described in detail the work or apostolate of the laity in the Church. Lay men and women ought "to take on as their distinctive task this renewal of the temporal order" (#7).

While it is not possible to determine the impact of these new emphases in Church teaching at each Catholic institution, it is fair to say that the change from religious leadership to lay leadership proceeded rather smoothly because lay leaders already associated with those institutions were ready to assume new and more responsible leadership positions.

Internal Pressures

In addition to the desire to be eligible to receive federal funds and to the desire to be accredited by the associations of higher education, other factors brought pressure to change. There were also internal pressures bubbling up within the institutions themselves. Consonant with all American institutions of higher education, Catholic colleges were experiencing great growth. Between 1960 and 1980 enrollment on Catholic campuses increased from approximately 231,000 to 609,000 students.[17] The sector of most growth was adult students. Colleges opened or expanded their evening courses, particularly in business and law, to accommodate working men and women seeking additional credentials to enhance job advancement. The number of women at institutions of higher education increased, as did the number of students of color, particularly from the African-American community. Increases in student population called for additional faculty, new academic programs, and often new or renovated facilities. These initiatives required more capital and more careful management. Colleges and universities turned to their lay advisors and friends to accomplish these goals.

[15] Vatican II, pastoral constitution, *Gaudium et spes*, December 7, 1965: *AAS* 58 (1966), 1025-1115.
[16] Vatican II, decree, *Apostolicam actuositatem*, November 18, 1965: *AAS* 58 (1966), 837-864.
[17] Gallin, *Negotiating Identity*, 47.

As the faculties of these institutions grew in number they also grew in their professionalism. They wanted the same rights and guarantees in employment and in governance as their peers enjoyed in public and other private institutions. Until the 1960s the issue of academic freedom had been dormant for Catholic colleges and universities. Up to that time, faculties at Catholic institutions were "free to teach provided their statements were not contrary to teaching of the Catholic Church or the Constitution of the United States."[18] Faculties now wanted their institutions to adopt the standard set by the American Association of University Professors (AAUP). Some faculties, dissatisfied with their lack of salary increases, the limitations on academic freedom and/or their rightful role in the governance of the colleges and universities, formed unions. All major issues concerning the faculty, e.g., salary, benefits, teaching loads, promotions, became part of the bargaining agreement. Some faculties, dissatisfied with the negotiations or the outcomes, went on strike.[19]

Students were also exerting pressure on the administration. As new ethnic and cultural groups grew larger, some student groups pushed for a voice in policy decisions. At times student groups pressed for funds to support their causes, some of which were in conflict with Catholic teachings and values. Administration had not been properly prepared for the issues and demands raised by these minority groups. Few if any members of the religious institute and the administration of the institutions of higher education were also members of these ethnic groups. Again, the administration looked to and needed the wisdom, expertise and guiding hand of their lay colleagues and experts.

On the Brink of Change

Changes in the governance of Catholic colleges and universities were inevitable. The classic model of the previous era was not sufficient. The lay men and women who served in increasing numbers on boards of trustees were often unacquainted with the nuances of canon law. At times the canonical permissions necessary for alienation of property and for assuming debt appeared too cumbersome for the needs of an efficient and timely process. In addition, the procedure of seeking government loans required some collateral. It was not advisable for all property to be held in the name of the religious sponsor, rather than in the name of the institution.

[18] Ibid., 59.

[19] The faculty of St. John's University went on strike in December 1965. The AAUP formally censured St. John's in June 1966.

Presidents of colleges and universities were faced with numerous challenges. How could they separate the governance structure of the institution from the governance structure of the religious order and still remain connected to the charism of the religious institute? How could they demonstrate that their colleges and universities were "secular" enough to attract federal funding and still maintain their Catholic identity? If they invited members of the laity onto their boards in such numbers as to have the majority vote, what would be the impact on the control exercised by the leadership of the religious institute. What were the consequences of such actions at both civil and canon law?

McGrath Thesis

Msgr. John J. McGrath, both a canon and civil lawyer, was an associate professor of comparative law at The Catholic University of America who had undertaken a legal study of American Catholic colleges and universities and other Catholic institutions. He lectured widely to the higher education community and, in 1968, published his findings and opinions in a monograph entitled *Catholic Institutions in the United States: Canonical and Civil Law Status*. This work became known as the McGrath thesis.

McGrath began his essay with a series of questions.

> If laymen [sic] constitute the majority of the governing board, is the institution still Catholic? Is church property being alienated when a majority of laymen [sic] are elected to the board and thus have effective control of the institution? In attempting to fulfill the mandate of Vatican Council II to use lay people in their proper role in our institutions, are we not violating the canon law of the same Church? Who really owns our Catholic institutions? What law governs them, canon law or civil law?[20]

The McGrath thesis has been summarized in this way:

> At the moment of an apostolate's civil incorporation, the incorporated institution ceased to be ecclesiastical goods. It was civil law that caused this transformation, not canon law, and therefore canonical permission was not necessary for the civil restructuring.[21]

[20] John J. McGrath, *Catholic Institutions in the United States: Canonical and Civil Law Status* (Washington, DC: The Catholic University of America Press, 1968) 1.

[21] Daniel C. Conlin, "The McGrath Thesis and its Impact on a Canonical Understanding of the Ownership of Ecclesiastical Goods." *CLSA Proceedings* 64 (2002) 83.

McGrath arrived at this conclusion by asserting that when a Catholic institution was civilly incorporated it became a legal entity independent from its sponsoring religious organization. As a charitable, non-profit corporation, these institutions had the duty to serve the general public. He further contended that the Catholic institution itself, not the sponsoring body, held legal title to all property and assets. However, there is an "equitable title" to the same assets. Because a charitable corporation that holds the legal title to property does not have any stockholders, the equitable title is held by the general public who receive benefit from the business of the corporation.

McGrath's study of corporate charters and by-laws of many Catholic educational institutions demonstrated that they had not been formally erected as moral persons according to canon law through appropriate decrees. Consequently they could not be considered the property of the Church or their sponsoring religious institute and, further, the administration of this property did not need to follow the norms of canon law. He concluded:

> The canon law is clear that property is ecclesiastical only when it belongs to some ecclesiastical moral person. Since the institutions under consideration (Catholic hospitals and higher education institutions) have not themselves been established as moral persons and, since no other moral person in fact holds title to the property of the institution, their assets are not ecclesiastical property."[22]

Even if such ecclesiastical action had been taken after the civil incorporation, McGrath held that it would have no real juridical effect.[23] Only civil authority could change the legal nature of the institutions.

Harrington summarizes the recommendations that McGrath offered as a consequence to his observations.

> ...the best way to legally insure that the sponsoring religious order can continue to participate actively in the affairs of the institution is to include in its bylaws provisions requiring that the president or other leaders of the institution be members of the order or that a specified number of seats on the board be appointed by the order; that given the nature of these institutions as 'public trusts,' their governing board should include laymen [sic] whose interests and abilities appropriately reflected the various constituencies served by the institutions; that the property and finances of the institution and the religious order

[22] McGrath, 24.
[23] McGrath, 18.

be kept completely separate and be managed independently; and that faculty who are members of the religious order should be paid full salaries and be subject to the same employment terms as other employees...[24]

Influence of McGrath Thesis

Catholic colleges and universities had already begun to make changes in their governance structure to address the needs of the institutions. The McGrath thesis gave them the canonical justification they needed to transform their boards of trustees into predominately lay boards that would have full legal governing power. There was no need to seek ecclesiastical permission for such a move because, according to McGrath, the property acquired by the institution was not ecclesiastical property and was owned by the corporate entity.

In 1967 St. Louis University reconstituted its board of trustees by inviting eighteen lay men and women, nine of them Catholics and nine of other faiths to join five Jesuits. Before making the final decision, Paul Reinert, S.J., St. Louis University president, consulted with many experts including the Jesuit General Superior in Rome and Joseph Cardinal Ritter, Archbishop of St. Louis. In the end, the decision was implemented with no indult or permission for alienation of ecclesiastical property. By contrast, the University of Notre Dame, thinking that the university was indeed ecclesiastical property, sought and obtained an indult of alienation for its restructuring in 1967.[25] Many Catholic colleges and universities in the United States followed the model offered by St. Louis University, not that of Notre Dame.

Critique of the McGrath Thesis

While there was little discussion of McGrath's monograph in legal journals, there were some negative voices heard early. James O'Connor, S.J., a canonist, reported to a meeting of Jesuit university presidents in 1966 that he thought the property of Catholic colleges was ecclesiastical property and that its administration was governed by canon law.[26] Robert White presented a paper at a conference held for officials of Jesuit institutions in the Maryland Province in May 1967. He held that the educational institution was an asset of the moral personality of the local religious community.[27] Similar reservations were

[24] Harrington, 61.
[25] Gallin, *Independence and a New Partnership*, 112.
[26] Ibid., 107
[27] James J. Conn, *Catholic Universities in the United States and Ecclesiastical Authority* (Rome: Editrice Pontificia Universita Gresfariana, 1991) 200.

voiced by the leadership of the Congregation of the Holy Cross at their 1967 General Chapter.[28] The dissenting opinions did not change McGrath's thesis that was published shortly thereafter.

The first publicized critique of the McGrath thesis was by Adam Maida, a canon and civil lawyer in the chancery of the Diocese of Pittsburgh. Maida unfavorably reviewed McGrath's work in 1973.[29] According to Maida, under canon law Catholic institutions are either moral persons or are church property owned by moral persons and therefore fall under the authority of the canons concerning administration. He contended that civil law incorporation does not take away the moral personality of these institutions. Two years later, Maida authored a booklet commissioned by the Pennsylvania Catholic Conference.[30] While not explicitly mentioning the McGrath thesis, he gave several arguments to demonstrate that Catholic institutions are ecclesiastical moral persons or share in such a moral personality. Therefore, he argued, they are subject to Church laws governing the administration and alienation of property owned by juridic persons.

Part of Maida's argument was itself the target of critique. For example, according to noted canonists James Coriden and Frederick McManus, Maida put too exclusive an emphasis on control by the bishops or religious superiors. In bypassing other canonical institutes, such as diocesan consultors, provincial councils and other administrators of church property, Maida neglected the canonical structures intended to restrain unitary power.[31]

The McGrath thesis was finally repudiated by the Holy See. In a January 2, 1974 letter to Archbishop Jean Jadot, the Apostolate Delegate in the United States, Gabriel-Marie Cardinal Garrone, Prefect of the Sacred Congregation for Catholic Education, requested the Delegate's opinion about a possible joint letter with the Sacred Congregation for Religious and Secular Institutes on the "status of the property and name of the many Catholic colleges and universities

[28] Gallin, *Independence and a New Partnership*, 113.

[29] Adam J. Maida, "Canonical and Legal Fallacies of the McGrath Thesis on Reorganization of Church Entities," *The Catholic Lawyer* 19 (1973) 275-286.

[30] Adam J. Maida, *Ownership, Control and Sponsorship of Catholic Institutions: A Practical Guide* (Harrisburg, PA: Pennsylvania Catholic Conference, 1975).

[31] James A. Coriden and Frederick R. McManus, "The Present State of Roman Catholic Canon Law Regarding Colleges and Sponsoring Religious Bodies," *Church and Campus: Legal Issues in Religiously Affiliated Higher Education*, ed. Philip R. Moots and Edward M. Gaffney (Notre Dame, IN: Notre Dame Press, 1979) 147. For more critique see Robert T. Kennedy, "McGrath, Maida, Michiels: Introduction to a Study of the Canonical and Civil-Law Status of Church-Related Institutions in the United States," *The Jurist* 50 (1990), 368-381.

in the United States."[32] Garrone indicated that the letter would prohibit the use of the McGrath thesis as a pretext for alienating property without first reference to the Holy See. There is no record of what advice Jadot might have given. On October 7, 1974 such a joint letter was sent to John Cardinal Krol, President of the National Conference of Catholic Bishops. It called for a joint commission to be set up to study the matter. The commission would have representatives from the National Conference of Catholic Bishops, the Conference of Major Superiors of Men and the Leadership Conference of Women Religious in the United States The letter clearly stated the opinion of the joint commission concerning the matter:

> We know that in the course of the study, the influence of the so-called 'McGrath thesis' will emerge as one of the principal bases for the action of some institutions in regard to alienation, etc. We wish to make it clear that this thesis has never been considered valid by our Congregations and has never been accepted.[33]

Apparently the joint commission held one meeting on January 24, 1975. It recommended that the NCCB should commission a comprehensive study on the ownership and control of Church property in the United States and should issue interim guidelines that would address the matters of ownership and control.[34] The American bishops adopted Maida's monograph and forwarded it to Rome as the interim guidelines called for by the joint commission.

Sponsorship after the McGrath Thesis

In 1977 Martin Stamm analyzed the governing documents of 134 Catholic colleges and universities. He reported that these institutions were employing three basic corporation governance systems, forming eight fundamental governance models.[35] Three schools did not have a separate corporation but shared the corporate identity of the parent corporation, and hence Stamm labeled this the corporate subsystems model. The sponsoring religious body exercised the corporate powers for the educational institution as well as for other apostolates.

[32] *Canon Law Digest*, 9: 368.
[33] *Canon Law Digest*, 9: 370.
[34] Kennedy, 366.
[35] Martin Stamm, "Emerging Corporation Models of Governance in Contemporary American Catholic Higher Education," *Current Issues in Catholic Higher Education* 2 (Summer, 1981) 38-45.

Nine colleges and universities were semi-independent corporations. While they had all the characteristics of a separate legal corporate entity, they were prescribed by their by-laws to seek formal approval or concurrence from some other corporation in order to perform one or more of the primary corporate functions.[36]

The other 122 colleges and universities fell into the independent corporate system model. There were two main types in this model, the uni-cameral and the bi-cameral. Sixty percent of all Catholic colleges and universities adopted the uni-cameral, independent model. This independent corporation is governed by a single corporate group, usually called the board of trustees or the board of regents, which exercises the power to implement decisions of all primary corporate responsibilities. Most of these governing bodies specified membership requirements for the sponsoring religious body, but reserved no specific powers reserved to them. Religious and lay members shared equally in the exercise of corporate responsibility.[37]

Forty-two colleges and universities had adopted the bi-cameral, independent corporate system model. Here there are two groups exercising corporate governance. Stamm identified five different modalities in this model. The type most commonly used (18% of all institutions) has an upper-echelon body and a lower-echelon body to which is delegated, shared or bestowed one or more primary corporate functions. Most often the upper-echelon body, sometimes called the Member, reserved complete power to exercise the corporation's primary responsibilities of disposition or acquisition of property or assets, altering the purpose/mission of the institution and amending the articles of the incorporation of the college or university. In many cases it was this Member group that selected and appointed members to the lower-echelon group or board.[38]

Canonical Stewardship

Unless the founding religious institute has formally alienated the property of its Catholic college or university, the religious institute remained the canonical administrator and steward of the ecclesiastical goods of this educational institution. The *Code of Canon Law* mandates nine specific duties that canonical stewards are to undertake.[39] As the canonical juridic person, the sponsoring body

[36] Ibid., 43.
[37] Ibid., 41.
[38] Ibid., 42.
[39] See c. 1284 §2.

fulfills these duties either directly or through delegation. These duties are performed through a series of corporate actions, often referred to as reserved powers.[40] By reserving certain corporate decisions to itself, the religious institute assures that the mission, values and direction of the college or university will remain faithful to the founding charism and its Catholic identity.

SPONSORSHIP TODAY

In the year 2000, Melanie Morey, Ed.D. and Dennis Holtschneider, C.M. published their study of Catholic colleges and universities to determine the relationship between the founding religious institutes and these institutions of higher education.[41] Seventy percent of college presidents and 65% of leaders of religious institutes responded to the survey. This represented 172 or 85% of Catholic colleges and universities sponsored by religious institutes in the United States.

The research discovered that just under half of the colleges and universities (77) operate with a uni-cameral structure while the others (88) have a bi-cameral structure. This is a significant increase of the two-tier structure since the 1977 Stamm study. Those institutions with a single board usually require a specific percentage (ranging from 25-33.3%) of the religious institutes' representation.[42]

The two-tier governance structure is usually comprised of a board of trustees whose members are both laity and a certain number or proportion of members of the sponsoring religious institute. The second body might be the religious institute's governing council, all members of the religious institute or certainly a majority of the institute's members.

Seventy-two percent of the colleges in the study reported that the religious institutes have reserved powers. While fifty-six different kinds of powers were reported, most have reserved the authority concerning administration of property, mission and identity, and significant changes in the articles of incorporation. Only 44% reserved the appointment and removal of trustees and even

[40] For further discussion, see F. Morrisey's article, "Various Types of Sponsorship", Chapter Two in the present volume.

[41] Melanie M. Morey and Dennis H. Holtschneider, "Relationship Revisited: Changing Relationships Between U.S. Catholic Colleges and Universities and Founding Religious Congregations," *Current Issues in Catholic Higher Education* 21 (Fall, 2000) 3-39.

[42] Ibid., 16.

less, 38%, reserve the power to appoint the president.[43] Only 29% of the institutes of higher education reported having sponsorship documents. Sponsorship documents usually are agreements established outside the provisions of the charter and by-laws that delineate the relationship between the educational institution and the sponsoring religious institute.

A more recent development on Catholic campuses is the establishment of an office of mission or Catholic identity. There are many names for this position, e.g. Mission Effectiveness or Sponsorship and Mission. This administrator, often a vice-president or director who regularly reports to the president, is charged with bringing the influence of the religious institute into the daily operation of the administration. By raising mission questions at critical times and by holding educational programs throughout the institute of higher education, this administrator can assist the college or university in deepening its Catholic identity and assuring that the founding charism flourishes. Interestingly enough, two colleges reported that on their campus this administrative office is held by a layperson.[44]

Sponsorship into the Future

The demographic changes in the number and age of women and men religious call for a new look at sponsorship of Catholic higher education. Institutes and provinces which have long served as canonical sponsors are now merging with other institutes and provinces which do not have colleges or universities among their apostolates. With fewer members of religious institutes to carry out the functions of the sponsoring body, congregational leadership often does not wish to assume the responsibilities of canonical stewards.

Today there are members of sponsoring religious institutes dialoging with leadership of their colleges and universities about whether the religious institute wishes to or can continue as the canonical sponsor. After so many years, it is possible that the religious institute no longer feels able to continue as the sponsor of a college or university. If the sponsoring relationship were to be terminated, the college or university might itself become a public juridic person or seek another sponsoring body.

[43] Ibid., 17.
[44] Ibid., 21.

CHAPTER SEVEN

A Juridic Meaning of Sponsorship in the Formal Relationship between a Public Juridic Person and a Healthcare Corporation in the United States

MELANIE DIPIETRO, SC

Introduction

The focus of this paper is on the use of sponsor or sponsorship in two contexts with juridic[1] consequences: (1) a canonical and legal analysis of the authority of leaders of the public juridic person in the governance of a healthcare corporation that carries on the apostolate of the public juridic person in the secular sphere;[2] and (2) the use of the term "sponsorship" in the public and legal documents of the healthcare corporation. The juridic dimension is suggested in the reference to the formal relationship of the canonical entity to the

[1] Juridic means of, or relating to, law or its administration; legal. (Bryan A. Garner, *A Dictionary of Modern Legal Usage* (New York: Oxford University Press, 1989). Juridic is used in this text when referring to both canon law and American law. Canon law, Code of Canon law or Code and canonist refer to discussion of the 1983 *Code of Canon Law* as a distinct legal system. Lawyer or American law refers to secular law as a distinct legal system.

[2] This paper addresses only public juridic persons. The description of the corporation as the place where the apostolate is carried on in the secular sphere is taken from statutes of recently created public juridic persons succeeding to the healthcare apostolates of religious institutes. For a discussion of these statutes in the context of the topic of this paper see, Melanie DiPietro, "An Examination of the *Universitas Rerum* and the *Universitas Personarum* of New Public Juridic Persons Succeeding to the Healthcare Apostolates of Religious Institutes in the United States" (J.C.D. diss., Pontifical University of St. Thomas in Rome, 2004), 209-226 (*Successor Public Juridic Persons*).

legal entity in the general definition of sponsorship used for the articles in this book. In this paper, formal relationship means a juridic relationship.[3]

In this paper three practical suggestions will be direveloped: (1) In the canonical and legal analysis that leads to the design of the formal juridic relationship between the canonical entity and the American corporation, technical juridic language is more useful than the word sponsorship which lacks a commonly accepted juridic meaning.[4] Use of the term sponsorship in theological contexts and non-juridic contexts needs to be distinguished from use of the term in juridic contexts, that is, in creating the formal legal structure that secures a position for the leadership of a public juridic person in the American corporation. (2) Any meaning of the word sponsorship expressed in canonical terms must be consistent with the facts and American law applicable to healthcare corporations. (3) If the purposes of incorporation are to protect the religious institute and to provide the healthcare corporation with the advantages of separate corporate status, the word sponsor should not be used in public or legal documents that may be used in adversarial legal contexts.

The factual and legal foundation for these suggestions will be developed by (1) a comment on the role of language in canonical and American legal analysis, collectively referred to as a juridic analysis; (2) a brief reference to historical canonical writings addressing the relationship of a canonical entity to a corporation; (3) an overview of the evolution of the uses of sponsorship within the healthcare community, and (4) the identification of a few principles of American law relevant to the operation of healthcare corporations.

This paper concludes with two recommendations: (1) an alternative canonical analysis and meaning for sponsorship when used as a tool in juridic analysis; and (2) sponsorship, regardless of any definition, should not be used in legal corporate documents.

[3] The definition of sponsorship used for the articles in this book is as follows: Sponsorship of an apostolate or ministry is a formal relationship between a recognized Catholic organization and a legally formed entity, entered into for the sake of promoting and sustaining the Church's mission in the world.

[4] Robert Keely, "Canonical Aspects of Catholic Identity in the Institutional Setting", *CLSA Proceedings* 61 (Washington: Canon Law Society of America, 1999), 197-198.

THE ROLE OF LANGUAGE IN JURIDIC ANALYSIS

In order to understand the distinction being made between the utility of the word sponsor in an informal or a theological context from a formal, juridic contextual use, it is necessary to consider the importance of language in law, a practical science. A canonist's or lawyer's use of language often controls the starting point, the direction and the content of a juridic analysis. The legal meaning given to a term identifies the legal rights, privileges, and duties that a person has in relationship to another person or object within that specific legal system.[5] In the context of the relationship of the leadership of a public juridic person to the governance authority in a corporation,[6] the starting point and direction of the canonical and legal analysis as well as the language used in the analysis are vital because the approach to the analysis will identify the canonical interests of the public juridic person that are to be protected in the operation of American law. The language used has no instructive value to the analysts if it has no accepted juridic meaning. For language to be instructive, it needs to have a meaning in each legal discipline. Further, the language that bridges canon law and American law must convey the principles of canon law that need to be protected in the operation of American law. These canonical principles need to be connected to specific authority in American law. In the

[5] R.J. Henle, ed., *St. Thomas Aquinas, the Treatise on Law* [being Summa Theologiae I-II:QQ.90-97], Notre Dame, IN, University of Notre Dame Press,1993, 35: "[L]anguage is recognized as a medium, a system of signification, through which actors not simply describe but create a world." In analyzing political issues, Hajer suggested that the real political conflict is hidden in definitions imposed by groups. Their definitions determine which aspects of reality are discussed and which are hidden. See Maarten A. Hajer, "Discourse in Coalitions and the Institutionalization of Practice: The Case of Acid Rain in Britain," in *The Argumentative Turn on Policy Analysis and Planning*, ed. F. Fischer and J. Forester (Durham, NC: Duke University Press, 1993), 42-43. In discussing legal reasoning, Levi stated that in an important sense legal rules are never clear. If a rule had to be clear before it could be imposed, society would be impossible. Legal reasoning accepts the differences of view and ambiguities of words. The ambiguity of words in the American Constitution was intended to provide the capacity to relate to future contingencies. See Edward H. Levi, *An Introduction to Legal Reasoning* (Chicago: The University of Chicago Press, 1949), 1, 65. In the American systems, ambiguous words are given a legal consequence by courts in adjudication of a conflict.

[6] For simplicity, the discussion will refer to the relationship of the public juridic person to the healthcare corporation. However, this is not accurate. *The canonical entity (and especially, the corporation carrying on the business of the canonical entity)* does not relate to the corporation. More precisely, persons who hold specific leadership office in the public juridic person, as individuals, are given a position, usually as a member, in the corporation. It is important in legal analysis and documents to eliminate reference to the canonical entity (and the corporation carrying on its business) and to keep the members in a corporation identified as individuals. Eligibility for membership is defined by office held in the canonical entity.

context of the juridic or formal relationship of the canonical entity to the corporation, the legal analysis and the resulting conclusions usually involve four areas of canonical interest which correspond to technical legal issues in American nonprofit corporation law: (1) the apostolate relates to the legal purpose of the corporation; (2) the means to carry out the apostolate relates to the legal dedication of the property in the corporation to Catholic healthcare; (3) the public identity of the apostolate relates to the people empowered to govern the corporation; and (4) the legal applicability of the religious and ethical practices of the corporation as they relate to corporate organizational documents, state law and constitutional law. In addition, the starting point and the direction of the analysis will determine the objective legal criteria that will be used to evaluate how well a specific legal structure, often called in common parlance a new sponsorship model, provides protection for these areas.

The application of canon and American law to facts in concrete situations such as American healthcare corporations — that is, the identification of canonical duties and relationships and the creation of legal structures to protect those canonical relationships — requires precision of juridic language applied to specific facts. The application of law to facts is important in canon law[7] as well as in American law. Precise juridic language focusing on specific facts and specific authority in American law leads to a more nuanced and improved use of American law to effect a desired canonical result. Since canon law may apply in the healthcare corporation only if constitutionally required[8] the ultimate criteria for any sponsorship structure needs to be grounded in American law. Each legal system has different processes for enforcing rights and obligations among natural and legal persons subject to its jurisdiction. In the resolution of any conflict concerning the assets of a healthcare corporation or the exercise of governance authority, the American state corporation law will be determinative. Therefore, canonical concepts need to correlate with legal concepts found in authoritative references of American law.

When changing corporate documents and governance relationships within healthcare corporations that are subject to the jurisdiction of American law and not in the control of canonical authority, American law will be the vehicle to achieve the goals stated by the client. If the client uses a word such as sponsorship, that lacks a juridic meaning, it is difficult for an American lawyer to identify the American law that will protect canonical norms that are relevant to the situation. Therefore, one of the tasks of the canonist engaged by a client

[7] R. Barrett, "The Philosophical Presuppositions of the Code," *Periodica* 89 (2000), 505.

[8] See for example, 15 Pa.C.S. § 5107.

is to educate the American lawyer about the canonical system governing the status, obligations and responsibilities of public juridic persons in regard to the apostolate under dscussion. If the corporation is, in fact, a means by which the public juridic person carries out its apostolate in the secular sphere, the American lawyer needs to understand the interrelationship of several canonical norms governing the status of the juridic person and the apostolate in the name of the Church.[9] In this paper, this canonical relationship and the various canonical norms relevant to it, will be referred to as the canonical order or canonical system.

Canonical References to the Relationship of the Canonical Entity to an American Corporation

The significance of language in controlling the direction of a juridic analysis is illustrated by comparison between approaches to the relationship of a canonical entity to a corporation taken by earlier canonists and those taken by more contemporary canonists.

One of the American Church's first significant responses to the operation of American corporate law as it affected the canonical order occurred during the later part of the nineteenth century and the early twentieth century. At that time many parishes and dioceses used the corporation with a board of trustees as the structure to hold title to church property. The bishops soon learned that American corporate law vests significant legal authority in the directors / trustees and protects their exercise of independent judgment in governing the affairs of the corporation. This experience is referred to within American church history as the problem of trusteeism. Eventually the US bishops used knowledge of corporate law to protect the operation of canon law as can be seen from some subsequent mandates issued by the provincial and plenary Councils of Baltimore (1852-1884) (the Councils) regarding the use of corporations holding title for diocesan or parish property:

- Appointment of lay trustees was subject to the bishop's approval;
- The bishop's approval was necessary for the alienation of property through sale, lease, or mortgage;

[9] C. 116 § 1.

- All trustees were to understand and accept the ultimate authority of the bishops and the law of the Church in matters related to the administration of property and their use of civil-law power;
- Any *ex-officio* trustees (e.g., pastors) of the corporation served coterminously with their canonical office.[10]

These excerpts from the particular law of the Councils illustrate several juridic points relevant to this discussion of sponsorship: (1) the use of *ex-officio* positions in the corporation corresponding with the leadership authority in the canonical juridic person; (2) the focus on the internal operation of the corporation and the persons who exercise authority in the corporation; (3) the protection of canonical principles by recognizing the factual and legal consequences of incorporation and corporate law; and (4) the significant correlation between the Council mandates and the scope of powers reserved to Members of a corporation in contemporary state nonprofit corporation laws.[11] The particular law of the Councils focused on corporate control as determined by American law by coordinating canon and American law.

The limited canonical references to healthcare corporations found prior to the 1960s are in the dissertations that are part of the "Tenure of Church Property Series" at The Catholic University of America in Washington, D.C. In 1941, Benjamin F. Farrell wrote that hospitals and institutions not established as moral persons, but "conjoined" or "adjoined" to ecclesiastical personalities, were subject to higher canonical competent authority. Ecclesiastical authority extended to vigilance, supervision over matters of religion, moral conduct, administration of the sacraments, and administration of property.[12] Joseph J. Comyns wrote in 1942 that institutions not erected as moral persons were, therefore, not possessors of "strictly ecclesiastical property." Such institutions were still subject to visitation, which logically necessitates the power to

[10] During the later part of the nineteenth century and the early part of the twentieth century canonists were most concerned with the problems of episcopal control in the corporations being used to hold title of parish property known as "trusteeism." See Paul Daniello, "An Analysis of Canon 1499§ 2 of the 1917 Code and Canon 1256 of the 1983 Code and Modern American Civil Law as to the Ownership and Modes of Tenure of Ecclesiastical Goods in the United States of America" (J.C.D. diss., Pontificia Studiorum Universitas a Santo Thoma Aquinate Urbe, 1996), 121-131, 139-160,162.

[11] See for example, 15 Pa.C.S. § 5505; 5721; 5724; 5725; 5751; 5914; 5922; 5930. The use of *ex-officio* members provided a structure to incorporate the mandates of the Councils into corporate governance.

[12] Benjamin F. Farrell, "The Rights and Duties of the Local Ordinary of Women Religious of Pontifical Approval" (J.C.D. diss., Canon Law Studies, no.128, The Catholic University of America, 1941), 122-123.

correct defects and establish norms of administration.[13] Urban C. Wiggins, writing in 1956, acknowledged that the corporation as a private entity, not the Church as a spiritual entity, holds property. While viewing the corporation as absolutely distinct, he saw the corporation as a "handmaid" of the Church, having the same rights and liabilities as all other private corporations.[14] Some canonical commentators assumed that the healthcare corporation was simply a means of holding property for a religious community.[15]

While these references are too limited to support any conclusions, it is reasonable to suggest that at least implicitly, these canonists – and by extension the bishops – began their analysis by identifying the status of the canonical actor and then viewed the corporation's existence and the corporate activities as a means to achieve the purposes of the canonical actor. These canonists, albeit implicitly, distinguished between the canonical actor and the corporation as an actor. Praxis at that time clearly shows that the link between the corporation and the canonical entity, i.e., governance control, existed in fact and by canonical mandate. The governance control of the corporation by the leadership of the canonical entity began to change in the 1960s. Debate concerning church property and governance control in the corporation and the popularization of the use of sponsorship arose in the changing legal environment of the 1960s, an era which gave rise to the McGrath/Maida debate.[16]

[13] Joseph J. Comyns, "Papal and Episcopal Administration of Church Property" (J.C.D. diss., Canon Law Studies, no.147, The Catholic University of America, 1942), 77-78.
[14] Urban C. Wiggins, "Property Laws of the State of Ohio Affecting the Church" (J.C.D. diss., Canon Law Studies, no.367, The Catholic University of America, 1956), 72-75.
[15] Donald C. McLeash, "The Laws of the State of Texas Affecting Church Property" (J.C.D. diss., Canon Law Studies, no.405, The Catholic University of America, 1960), 63.
[16] See John McGrath, *Catholic Institutions in the United States: Canonical and Civil Law Status*, (Washington: The Catholic University of America, 1968) and Adam Maida, *Ownership, Control and Sponsorship of Church Institutions*, (Harrisburg, PA: Pennsylvania Catholic Conference, 1975). These short monographs are the basis for the McGrath/Maida debate and the ensuing controversy within the canonical community concerning the appropriate governance structures of corporations.

McGrath/Maida Debate Popularized Sponsorship

McGrath and Maida differed on two fundamental issues in regard to the relationship of the canonical entity to the corporation: (1) characterization of the property in the corporation as church property; and (2) the appropriate role of the leadership of the public juridic person in the governance of the corporation. McGrath held that the property in the healthcare corporation was not church property. He recommended that the major superior not be in a governance position and that other members of the religious institute have only a minority presence on the board of directors. On the other hand, Maida held that the property in the healthcare corporation was church property. Maida suggested the membership model corporation with the major superior and council vested with authority to control fundamental corporate issues.[17]

The concept of sponsorship became popular precisely because the starting point of McGrath and Maida in the now famous McGrath/Maida debate was basically advocacy and not an objective analysis. Each canonist based his advocacy position on one concept in the 1917 Code of Canon Law, *dominium*, which was narrowed to the ownership of church property. The language of ownership, a notion in private property law (and not relevant to Members in a nonprofit corporation) was and continues to be problematic.[18] No person or other corporation owns the charitable assets of a charitable corporation.

McGrath correctly stated that the religious institute did not have legal title and, therefore, did not own the corporation nor the property titled in the corporation. McGrath made excellent recommendations regarding separating the life of the sponsoring body from the corporation. He seemed to suggest that minority presence of members of the religious institute was sufficient to keep the corporation under the auspices of the religious institute.[19] Maida countered that the property in the corporation was church property. While McGrath focused on legal title, Maida argued around it. He acknowledged that most of the property was titled in the corporation and, therefore, owned by the corporation. However, Maida argued, the corporation was an implied moral person.[20] Therefore, in the conclusion that he drew, he acknowledged ownership of the property by the corporation. In his recommendations Maida

[17] Ibid.

[18] For a fuller analysis of this point, an alternate to ownership analysis and a fuller analysis of the reasoning of McGrath and Maida, see DiPietro, *Successor Public Juridic Persons*, 26-42; 268-324.

[19] McGrath, 19-38.

[20] Maida, 36, 43, 44, 47.

actually focused on corporate control, not ownership. If one reads Maida's work, one can find a recognition of an unarticulated starting point: the canonical role of the religious institute and the function of its apostolate. McGrath started with ownership. Maida simply followed McGrath and also made ownership his explicit starting point.

Though McGrath used the word sponsorship in his monograph, and Maida used sponsorship in his response to McGrath, each had a different juridic implication for the use of the term. From their monographs, one may conclude that for McGrath, sponsorship inferred participation in governance which he described as influence, and for Maida, sponsorship meant an explicit description of the Membership model of governance in which the major superior and council were the Members in the corporation, vesting governance authority of the corporation in the leadership of the religious institute. Maida focused on control, not influence. Through reserved powers, the Members control fundamental elements of the corporation such as its purpose, the use to which the assets are dedicated and the appointment of directors. These reserved powers track the language of many state corporation laws.[21]

The term sponsor is not found in state non-profit corporation laws that define the vesting of authority in Members or directors to govern a corporation. Neither McGrath nor Maida offered any definition for the term, but the difference between influence and control in the conclusions of each of their monographs is fairly clear. While there is a notable consensus among canonists that sponsorship is not a juridic term in canon law,[22] nonetheless, sponsorship continues to be used and the canonical analysis of ownership of property in the healthcare corporation (instead of some other characterization supported by a different canonical analysis) continues to influence the relationship known as sponsorship. The problem with ownership language and a canonical analysis based on ownership has been implicitly or explicitly recognized by

[21] See note 11, *supra*.
[22] Keely, 197-198.

several canonists.[23] The disconnect between an analysis starting with ownership and the facts of the American corporation has led to an evolution of the use of the term in juridic context to mean any number of things, not all of which are grounded in the language or principles of corporate law.

Current Trends in the Use of Sponsorship

Three trends appear in the current use of sponsorship in a juridic context. First, some canonists continue to equate "sponsorship", often qualified by "religious sponsorship", with governance. These canonists stress the importance of separating sponsorship functions from the actual activities that occur in the corporation by Members and directors. The operations of a corporation under the control of management responsible to directors are functions that occur in the corporation by the authority of American law, not by canonical authority. Clear distinctions are to be maintained between the canonical entity and the corporation. Language and visual representations should consistently separate the functions of each entity.[24]

[23] Frank Morrisey has recognized the difficulty with *dominium* in the context of healthcare corporations. See, F. Morrisey, "Canon 1295: Establishment of Lay Boards and Alienation of Property," in *Roman Replies and CLSA Advisory Opinions*, ed. F. Steven Pedone and James Donlon (Washington: CLSA, 1998), 98-100. See also Melanie DiPietro, Chap. 13, "Impact of Canon Law On Health Care Delivery," in *Hospital Contract Manual*, vol. 3, ed. Baker Hosteller and Robert Wolin (Gaithersberg, MD: Aspens Publisher, 2000); *Congregational Sponsorship: Issues In A Community Dialog* (Madison, WI: Catholic Health Association of Wisconsin,1985). Adam J. Maida and Nicholas P. Cafardi, Church *Property, Church Finances, and Church-Related Corporations: A Canon Law Handbook* (St. Louis, MO: The Catholic Health Association of the United States, 1984), 215. Robert Kennedy uses canonical ownership in "Note on the Canonical Status of Church-Related Institutions in the United States," in *New Commentary on the Code of Canon Law*, ed. John Beal et al. (New York; NY: Paulist Press, 2000), 176.

[24] Joy Conti, "Liability Issues for Related Church Entities," in *Acts of the Colloquium on Public Ecclesiastical Juridic Persons and Their Civilly Incorporated Apostolates in the Catholic Church in the U.S.A.: Canonical -Civil Aspects*. [no editor cited.] (Rome: Pontifical University of Saint Thomas Aquinas, 1998),101-179. Also J. Conti, "Anticipating and Avoiding Bankruptcy-Liability Exposure for Related Entities," in *The Administration of Church Property: A Jubilee International and Ecumenical Canon Law Conference*, ed. Joseph Fox, (Pittsburgh, PA: Duquesne University, The Law School, 2001), 293-298. See Melanie DiPietro, Chap. 13, "Impact of Canon Law On Health Care Delivery," in *Hospital Contract Manual*, vol. 3, ed. Baker Hosteller and Robert Wolin (Gaithersberg, MD: Aspens Publisher, 2000); *Congregational Sponsorship: Issues In A Community Dialog* (Madison, WI: Catholic Health Association of Wisconsin, 1985); "Organizational Overview," in *Who Do You Say We Are?* (Arlington, VA: Catholic Charities USA, 1997); Maida and Cafardi, 206-208.

Second, sponsorship is given many meanings which are vague and which lack any relationship to fundamental legal concepts in American corporation law. Some uses vaguely describe the canonical responsibility of the public juridic person for its assigned work. For example: "Sponsorship describes the relationship between an organization and a religious institute." "Sponsorship is a promise or a commitment or an enduring relationship over time." "Sponsorship formally organized the ministry to be a call to healing presence." "Sponsorship is a corporate commitment to keep the ministry going." "Sponsorship is whatever you want to create."[25]

Third, some commentators introduced new models of sponsorship such as the "influence model" which obviously is inconsistent with a control model.[26] This period also included the development of co-sponsorship models. Sometimes in co-sponsorship models, perhaps because of the moral person/ownership approach, the leadership of the religious institute usually retained the authority to approve encumbrances and transfers of property of the corporation. Different classes of Members with different kinds of authority in the corporation exercise other reserved powers. Such division of authority may not protect the canonical duties of the major superior and council because of the way in which specific state statutory provisions vest rights and authority in Members.[27] Sometimes, one class of Members may represent all of the co-sponsors. Usually, each sponsor appoints some portion of this representative class of Members. This new representative class often exercises reserved powers originally held by the individual sponsor. Thus the authority to encumber or alienate assets may be in one body and the authority to modify or change the purpose for which the property is dedicated may be in another body.

In other situations, the powers that were retained by Members were often further modified to be the *approval* or *ratification* authority. In this case, the power

[25] See for example, Lawrence E. Singer, "Realigning Catholic Health Care: Bridging Legal and Church Control in a Consolidating Market", *Tulane Law Review* 72:159 at note 68.

[26] The influence model of sponsorship was a topic of "Fourth-Generation Sponsorship: Moving to Influence", a conference held by the Center for Catholic Health Care and Sponsorship of Loyola University School of Law, Institute for Health Law, March 26, 1996. (The information from this conference is available from Lawrence Singer, director, Center for Catholic Health Care and Sponsorship, Loyola University School of Law, Chicago, IL.) See also, Beverly K. Dunn, *Apostolate: Procedural Handbook for Institutes of Consecrated Life and Societies of Apostolic Life* (Washington: CLSA, 2001), 184-187.

[27] For example, in some circumstances amendments to Articles of Incorporation changing rights of classes of members may require the consent of the class. See Pa. C.S.A. § 5914.

of Members to act amounts to a veto, thus divesting from the Members the powers to initiate and effect a corporate action. In such a situation, if the Members want to join a larger corporation, such an action may be difficult to implement unless the board votes first to amend corporate documents to effect the transaction. In addition, *delegation* language is sometimes introduced into civil law documents such as the bylaws. The use of delegation concepts are not commonly found in state non-profit corporation statutes because such delegation may be inconsistent with fiduciary duties. Some novel structures actually created in corporate documents may not be provided for explicitly in state statutes.[28]

In addition, at times sponsorship agreements, in lieu of the governance structures created by state statutes, are used. These sponsorship agreements or contracts often address philosophy and Catholic identity and create communication between the corporation and the religious institute. However, as a contracting party, the religious institute may have no right to participate in governance even if stated in the contract unless there is specific legislation that permits a body outside the corporation to exercise governance authority in the corporation.[29] The enforceability of these agreements or actual remedies for the breach of such agreements depends upon state law and the terms of the contract.

Finally, use of the term sponsorship without a factual basis in canonical and legal analysis has led, in many instances, to being simply an influence or presence of the public juridic person in governance as an equally acceptable alternative to a control model of sponsorship.

One simple example illustrates the problem with accepting influence or presence as a juridic meaning of sponsorship. If influence and presence are acceptable juridic interpretations of sponsorship, and these have no protection in American law, the ability of public juridic persons to initiate and complete transactions such as the development of health care systems or the creation of successor public juridic persons and the transfer of governance authority in the corporation to a canonical successor may be seriously jeopardized, if not

[28] This author has had conversation with legal colleagues who created sponsorship structures not explicitly provided for in a specific state statute. When questioned concerning the protection of the statute for such a structure, the colleague responded that the structure may not, in fact, be authorized by the state statute. After advising his client of the risk, it was his opinion that contract law, not non-profit corporation law may protect the intended relationship of the parties. Contract law may be applicable to bylaws which regulate the internal affairs of the corporation. However, private agreements contrary to the state statutory scheme controlling the action of a corporation may not be enforceable. See, for example, *Seven Springs Farm, Inc. v. Croker*, 569 Pa. 202,801 A.2d 1212 (2002).

[29] Some state statutes may explicitly allow an "Other Body" to exercise authority normally vested by the state statute in Members or Directors. See Pa.C.S.A. § 5103.

impossible. For example, if the Members have only veto power or have only influence or presence, they have no authority to initiate and effect corporate reorganizations creating a system or to transfer governance authority in the corporation to a canonical successor unless the action is initiated and proposed by the directors to the Members or agreed to by a majority of the directors. The creation of a public juridic person pertains solely within the jurisdiction of canon law. However, the stable, legal connection of the public juridic person to the means necessary to carry out the apostolate that are titled in the corporation is achieved only by action of the corporation; this action is taken by the Members and/or directors who control the Articles of Incorporation and other powers in the corporation. The transfer of control from one group to another, which may be accomplished by amendments to Articles of Incorporation and bylaws, is controlled by state law.

Sponsorship, an isolated term without canonical frame of reference and with a potentially negative use in American law,[30] either needs to be given a meaning explained in a canonical analysis using canonical language that can be related to American law or to be avoided in juridic analysis. The disconnect between the meanings of sponsorship as influence or presence and the operation of American law is illustrated by a short discussion of the American law governing nonprofit corporations.

American Law Relevant to the Juridic Use of Sponsorship

The first Supreme Court decision to address Catholic hospitals was the 1899 *Bradfield* case, in which the term "under the auspices of" was used referring to the relationship of the Sisters of Charity (now Daughters of Charity) to Providence Hospital in Washington, D.C.[31] The controversy in *Bradfield* was a First Amendment challenge to the government's purchase of services from a hospital corporation completely controlled by Roman Catholic sisters.

Bradfield clearly separated the corporation as the legal actor in the secular environment from the religious institute, regardless of the fact that only sisters exercised civil corporate control. The *Bradfield* decision specifically stated that hospital property, regardless of the identity of the trustees of the corporation, is not held in trust for a religious institute nor was it subject to ecclesiastical

[30] See, *Barr v. Methodist Home*, 90 Cal. App.3d 259,153 Cal. Rptr. (1979).

[31] *Bradfield v. Roberts*, 175 U.S. 291 (1899).

supervision. The *Bradfield* decision accepted and did not challenge control of the hospital by an all sisters board. This distinction between ownership and control is very important, especially in light of the ownership language which continues to be used in contemporary canonical analysis.[32]

The legal significance of the distinction between the language of ownership of property and control of a corporation is illustrated by the following language of early corporate charters and the legal principles enunciated in a seminal Supreme Court decision. The language of an 1898 incorporation charter (Articles of Incorporation) indicated that the incorporators (religious superiors) received the following powers in the healthcare corporation.

> ...all powers usually exercised by stockholders including the power to *elect directors*, make bylaws and they shall exercise *all the powers* of every description which under the laws are vested in the corporation.[33] (Emphasis added)

This language concerns the exercise of powers of the corporation itself and the power to govern the internal affairs of the corporation. The language is not that of ownership. The power of the incorporator is compared to a stockholder but the incorporator is not a stockholder. Earlier in the 1819 Supreme Court decision in *Trustees of Dartmouth College v. Woodward*,[34] the Court held that a charter enjoys constitutional protection as a contract between the state and the corporation. The current documents in American law which evidence these contractual rights are the state law and the articles of incorporation.[35]

After incorporation, the powers granted to the incorporators are exercised by members. Many state laws accord the type of authority vested in the incorporators, quoted above in the original charter, to members. Contemporary statutory rights of members include the authority to amend the articles of

[32] See Robert Kennedy, "Note on the Canonical Status of Church-Related Institutions in the United States," in *New Commentary on the Code of Canon Law*, ed. John Beal et al. (New York, NY: Paulist, 2000), 176. See also, Daniel Conlin, "Canonical and Civil Legal Issues Surrounding the Alienation of Catholic Health Care Facilities in the United States" (J.C.D. diss., Pontifical University of St. Thomas Aquinas, 2000).

[33] Archives, Sisters of Charity of Seton Hill, Greensburg, PA. #A-704. Application for Charter and Charity Hospital Charter, In the Court of Common Pleas No. 3 of Allegheny County, PA No. 195, February Term, 1898. The right of incorporators and subsequently of members to elect directors is now codified in many state statutes.

[34] *Trustees of Dartmouth College v. Woodward*, 17 U.S. 518 (1819).

[35] See for example, *Harbison v. Strickland*,2004 WL 2367837 (Ala.) So. 2d. *Aztec Motel, Inc. v. State ex. rel. Faircloth*, 251 So. 2d 849 (1971).

incorporation and approve fundamental corporate reorganizations. If there are no members, these powers are, by state law, vested in the directors. If the members modify the powers vested in members by state law, those powers usually are irrevocably vested in the directors, unless directors are willing to reinvest members with the authority they previously divested.

Corporate existence, its capacity to act and the authority of Members and directors to govern a corporation are all created by a positive authorization of the state expressed in the state statute creating corporations. The corporation can only exercise its powers through Members and directors.[36] A specific corporation's powers and authorized purposes are found in its Articles of Incorporation. So, too, the authority to govern the corporation, vested in either Members or directors is found in the Articles of Incorporation and bylaws of a specific corporation. The Articles of Incorporation and bylaws are valid only if consistent with the state law.[37] Consequently, structures of governance that are not within the authorization of the state statutes, governance disputes between Members and directors, disputes concerning the use of corporate assets, and disputes involving contracts between Members and the corporation will be examined and judged in the context of the Articles of Incorporation read in connection with the state statute.[38] If the Articles of Incorporation or a particular contract are not consistent with the state law, the state law prevails over the private agreement.[39] The state law, the corporate documents that are in compliance with the state law and the legal principles of the cases cited are the bases in American law that provide protection for the canonical interests in (1) the statement of purpose of the corporation; (2) the dedicated use of the property of the corporation; (3) the identity of those who govern the corporation; and (4) legal protection for the ethical mandates governing the activities of the corporation.

[36] 18 Am Jur 2d §§1,2.(2004).
[37] See *Harbison v Strickland*, 2004 WL 2367837 (Ala.), 6.
[38] Ibid.

Some Popular Meanings of Sponsorship Not Grounded in State Law

The general legal principles stated above applicable to the activities and governance of corporations provide the legal context in which the corporation, the public juridic person, canonists and American lawyers must work. This reality suggests the weakness of a canonical analysis that continues to use sponsorship in a juridic context without grounding it in the facts of the operation of a corporation and in the language of canon law and American law. This legal reality also suggests that ownership of property is not the right starting point of the juridic analysis. American law and the applicability of the general principles described above lead to a certain logical conclusion. If the corporation is the place in the secular sphere where the canonical actor carries out its apostolate, the corporate structure needs to be one that is authorized by and consistent with the state non-profit corporation law. Regardless of the intention of the parties, the state statute defines the persons in the corporation who have vested governance authority. Influence or presence are simply not models of corporate governance. Those who have governance authority in the corporation, as defined in the state statute and exercised in accord with the provisions concerning such matters as quorums and majority vote, can alter such presence or influence at will. This fact creates an interesting challenge to the relationship of the public juridic person to the corporation that theoretically carries on its apostolate in the secular sphere. How can the canonically responsible person be present in the corporation at the will of third parties? By this same logic, sponsorship agreements with no substantive enforceable rights are also inadequate. In a dispute, the court's frame of reference is American law. Canon 1284[40] requiring the observance of civil laws so that no harm comes to the Church from non-observance of secular law, and requiring that the claim to church property be supported by documents and records, can be observed only by working through established principles of American law when using the term sponsorship in juridic contexts or when creating new sponsorship models.

[39] See *Seven Springs Farm, Inc. v. Croker* 569 Pa. 202,801 A.2d 1212.

[40] C.1284 § 1, § 2.3° and 9°.

Recommendation One: A Different Starting Point for a Meaning for Sponsorship

Given the facts of either the incorporation or acquisition of the healthcare corporation originally by the superiors of religious institutes,[41] or currently by Catholic hospitals and the legal principles summarized above, an alternative canonical analysis and a more precise meaning for sponsorship used in a juridic context is offered. The starting point of this canonical analysis, giving a meaning of sponsorship in a juridic context, is not ownership of property.[42] Rather it is the status of the canonical actor and the necessary connection between the purpose of the canonical actor and the means, in the reality of the specific legal and factual situation, to fulfill its apostolic purpose.[43]

Description of the Canonical Order

The recommended canonical analysis, expressed in canonical language that more closely tracks the canonical order while still being consistent with the facts and law relevant to the operation of American healthcare corporations is as follows. The starting point is the canonical actor, a public juridic person, who exercises its proper work (c. 675 §3) or designated apostolic work (c. 114 §§1 and 2) in the name of the Church and in communion with the Church (c. 116 §1). Second, a public juridic person needs to have the means, sufficient in the specific circumstances of its apostolate, to achieve its apostolic purpose (c. 114 § 3). Third, the temporal goods acquired by a public juridic person to carry out its purpose, acquired by a legitimate and just means in civil law, are considered as church property to be administered in accord with the law of the Church (cc. 1254 and 1259). Fourth, in fact the corporation and its temporal and human

[41] For a description of three different factual incorporation experiences from 1899 to 1954, see *Successor Public Juridic Persons*, 60-74. See also William W. Bassett, "The American Civil Corporation, the 'Incorporation Movement' and the Canon Law of the Catholic Church," in *Journal of College and University Law*, 25 (1999), 721-750.

[42] For an explanation of the canonical characterization of property in the corporation based on contract analysis, see *Successor Public Juridic Persons*, 162-195.

[43] See, for example, the analysis of canons 113-116 in terms of the purpose of the actor and the means to fulfill its end in Julio Garcia Martin, *Le norme generali del Codex Iuris Canonici*, 3rd ed. (Roma: Ediurcla, 1999), 391-399. Canon 114 requires that the purpose of the juridic person pertain to the apostolate, that it be useful and that the juridic person have the means sufficient to fulfill the purpose. Canon 116 states that the public juridic person is given a purpose by competent authority and is authorized to fulfill its purpose in the name of the church.

resources are the means by which the public juridic person carries on its apostolate in the secular sphere (c.114 § 3). The canonical actor needs to have a stable legal connection to those resources that are, from a canonical perspective, the means used to carry out the apostolate. Fifth, canon 1290 accepts the American law of contracts. Sixth, authentic copies of the documents and records that are the basis for the claims of the public juridic person in relation to the means, temporal goods, used to carry on the apostolate are to be safeguarded by the public juridic person (c.1284 § 2.9°). Seventh, the rights to the temporal goods which pertain to the public juridic person for use in its apostolate are to be protected by appropriate civil law means. (c.1284 §2.3°).

American Legal Principles Relevant to the Canonical Order

The application of this canonical order to the facts of the formal relationship of the public juridic person to the healthcare corporation to American law rests on four facts: 1) the actor in the secular sphere is the corporation; 2) the corporation is the means in the secular sphere to carry on the healthcare apostolate; 3) the religious superiors or other authorities incorporated hospitals with the intention of carrying out their proper work; and, 4) the canonical actor needs to have an ongoing, stable connection to the means necessary to carry on its apostolate. The principles of American law relevant to these facts and the above described canonical order are as follows. First, the rights and powers granted to incorporators through the act of incorporation are the legitimate means in American law granted to persons to stabilize and carry on charitable works. Second, the rights granted in the charter to the incorporator and the corporation are constitutionally protected contracts. Third, the authentic documents which evidence the perpetual rights of the corporation to exist and to carry on activities in furtherance of its approved purposes and of the rights of members and directors to govern the corporation are found in the state law and the articles of incorporation and bylaws of the corporation. Fourth, the civil law method of protecting these contractual rights and the canonical order described above is secured by carefully written articles of incorporation and bylaws and by the use of internal governance structures that are clearly within the state statutory scheme. Fifth, in American law, through the act of incorporation, the incorporator and the subsequent members (if no members, the directors) exercise the powers of the corporation as vested in each body by the state statute. The members, as long as they are members, have the powers currently granted to members in state law unless the members have modified or forfeited them. Sixth, the state statute usually vests the following authority in members: 1) the statement of the purpose[44] of the corporation identifying the dedication of the property of the corporation to the purpose of the corporation; 2) the members' appointment of directors; 3) approval of fundamental corporation reorganizations; and, 4) dispositions of substantial assets of the corporation.[45] Since the documents that define the right of public juridic persons in relation to the corporation are the articles of incorporation and the bylaws both read in conjunction with the state statute, the legal language that is appropriate to use in protecting the canonical order is the language of corporation law. This language is vested authority as defined by the state statute, not simply influence.

The American lawyer meets the mandate of canon 1284 §3 by using these principles to provide the leadership of the public juridic person with authority in the corporation sufficient to protect all of the elements of the canonical order described above. The structure and scope of this internal authority should track the authority vested in members by the state statute. The corporate structure used must protect the ongoing ability of the canonical actor to exercise authority in the corporation to direct the means in the corporation to the purpose of the apostolate.

In the practical realm, the canonical order and the American legal principles suggest, at a minimum, the following norms: (1) the vesting of appropriate authority in the leadership of the public juridic person in the corporation; (2) control by the public juridic person of the purpose statement and dissolution clause in the articles of incorporation that permanently dedicates the assets acquired by the corporation to Catholic healthcare; (3) appropriate authority of leadership of the public juridic person in the corporation to identify those who govern the corporation; and, (4) appropriate provisions in corporate documents asserting the religious and ethical norms which govern the activities of the corporation. If a non Membership model of governance is used, or if there is an attempt to replace corporate structures with contracts, these basic elements of the canonical order need to be protected through the operation of American law.

[44] See note and text, at note 11 *supra*. The statement of purpose is required in the Articles of Incorporation. See "The Revised Model Nonprofit Corporation Act" adopted by the Subcommittee on the Model Nonprofit Corporation Law of the Business Law Section American Bar Association, 1987, §2.02.

[45] See note 11, *supra*.

A Meaning of Sponsorship in Juridic Contexts

Therefore, within this analytical approach to the design of the formal, that is juridic, relationship of the public juridic person to the healthcare corporation, the following is suggested as a juridic understanding of sponsorship.

Sponsorship is the legally protected authority in the corporation of the leadership of a public juridic person to control those elements of the corporation that correspond to the canonical order governing the relationship of a public juridic person to its apostolate.

Simply put, the canonical actor needs to maintain an appropriate control of the means necessary in the secular sphere to carry on its apostolate. At the same time, it must be noted that vigilance is required in this proposed meaning of sponsorship as a tool of juridic analysis. This alternative definition focuses on the appropriate exercise of authority *in the corporation* so that Members and directors get the benefit of the protection from personal liability and indemnification found in many state nonprofit corporation laws.[46]

The criteria used to identify these rights of the public juridic person or the type of formal relationship[47] between the public juridic person and the corporation that is necessary to protect the canonical order needs to be based in the American legal statutes and authoritative law that confers the rights in the corporation and regulates the exercise of those rights. If the language or the structure used in the documents creating the formal, juridic relationship is not grounded in American law, such language should not be used as a meaning for sponsorship.

[46] Legal counsel needs to be consulted to determine the position, description of qualification of Members or directors, and the appropriate division of authority between Members and directors and the appropriate language to state their authority. Real and substantial authority to manage the corporation needs to be vested in directors who exercise independent judgment.

[47] See, at note 3 *supra*.

Recommendation Two: Use of Sponsorship in Corporate Documents

The above analysis has stressed the positioning of the leadership of the public juridic person in the corporation. All activity of the leadership of the public juridic person needs to take place in the corporation in accord with corporate law so that the statutory provisions such as those protecting Members from liability solely by reason of being a Member or providing indemnification are applicable to their actions in the corporation. It is also necessary to separate clearly and consistently the life and interests of the religious institute from those of the corporation. They are two separate actors. The corporation is the only actor in the secular sphere that is involved in healthcare.

Documents such as letterhead and public relations materials describing the corporation should not use the word "sponsor". The organizational charts of the healthcare corporation should also avoid inclusion of any graphic representation of the religious institute or of the corporation carrying on the business of the religious institute. Rather, corporate documents and publications should be clear that the corporation is the independent legal actor. It is better to say that the corporation operates within a certain religious tradition than to say that it is sponsored by a distinct external religious entity. In a lawsuit involving Methodist Homes, the plaintiffs used the word sponsor that appeared in the corporation's documents as the basis to include the affiliated religious body as a defendant in a lawsuit against the corporation based on a contract between the residents and the Home.[48] The fact situation in this case suggests that it is good practice to be very clear to separate the religious institute from the activities in the corporation, both in practice and in corporate documents. This is done by using language carefully. It is also necessary to be clear that individuals, not the religious entity, are Members retaining only necessary reserved powers and vesting real and substantial authority in the Board of Directors. It is also helpful in the Articles of Incorporation and any financial documents and other such corporate documents to state clearly that the contractual obligations are solely those of the corporation.

[48] See *Barr v. United Methodist Church* 90 Cal.App.3d 259,153 Cal. Rpt.322 (1979).

Conclusion

The use of sponsorship in juridic contexts that is not grounded in fact and not given a meaning articulated in canonical and legal terminology permits novel structures like influence and presence to become acceptable. This approach to the formal relationship between the canonical entity and the corporation will contribute to the unraveling, albeit silently and imperceptibly, of the system or healthcare corporations formally related to public juridic persons. The irony is that the use of words like "influence" and "presence" as a juridic meaning of sponsorship invite a renewed McGrath/Maida debate not on ownership but on governance.

CHAPTER EIGHT

SPONSORS AND SPONSORED MINISTRIES: MUTUAL EXPECTATIONS

PATRICIA SMITH, OSF

Despite recent attempts to define or more accurately describe sponsorship, it remains an evolving concept embracing a plethora of models in the Catholic Church in the United States.[1] Frequently the remark is heard that if we have encountered one model of sponsorship we are knowledgeable of just that: one model. In light of its evolutionary nature no single snapshot of sponsorship actually exists; rather the concept can be imaged as a collage or a scrapbook containing various representations and continually in the process of being fashioned. Yet, regardless of the structure, whether the sponsors are religious,[2] lay or clerical, or a combination of any of these groups; whether a ministry is sponsored solely by one group, or is co-sponsored by two or more entities; whether the ministry shares the juridic personality of the sponsor or is itself a public juridic person; there are commonalities of what sponsors can and should share with sponsored ministries. Correspondingly there are expectations that

[1] In June 2005 the authors of this publication concurred on a juridic description of sponsorship based on a definition formulated by the Catholic Health Association (CHA). It states: "Sponsorship of an apostolate or ministry is a formal relationship between a recognized Catholic organization and a legally formed entity entered into for the sake of promoting and sustaining the Church's mission in the world." Although this description (and that of CHA) provides a common foundational base to aid in sponsorship discussions, they currently exist along side of numerous other definitions and descriptions created by various sponsors.

[2] For purposes of this chapter, unless otherwise implied, the term "lay" will be used in an exclusive sense to refer to those non-clerical members of the Church who are not members of a religious institute, a secular institute or a society of apostolic life.

sponsored ministries should have of their sponsors.[3] This chapter will focus on these mutual expectations.

The term "sponsored ministry" embraces an array of understandings that range from those in which the sponsors or members of the corporation have nominal involvement in the oversight of the ministry to those totally controlled by the sponsors. "Sponsored ministry" as used in this chapter implies the ministry or institution itself – a health care system, a college or school, a social service entity, a spiritual or environmental center, etc., that is a juridic person or shares in the juridic personality of another group. More specifically "sponsored ministry" will refer to those to whom the representatives of the juridic person entrust the governance and administration of the entity/institution, specifically the board of trustees and the senior management/ administrative team.[4] At indicated times "sponsored ministry" will also be used in its broadest sense, to include all those who are involved in the ministry in any capacity.

Before examining expectations it is essential to understand that faith is central to the relationship between the sponsors and the sponsored ministry. The sponsored ministry by its very existence is rooted in the Catholic faith tradition and is thus understood as a ministry of the Church.[5] Those who assist in governing or administering the institution must recognize its integral relationship in communion with the Church. Thus they need to possess a basic knowledge and understanding of the Catholic faith and exhibit a willingness to uphold and support it. Nourishing faith is the starting point of what sponsors are expected to share with sponsored ministries.

Essentially the sponsor invites those in the ministry to work with them in the name of the Church. This invitation is in keeping with the call of the Second Vatican Council, especially as voiced in *Gaudiem et spes* and *Apostolicam actuositatem*. Since both the sponsors and the sponsored ministry share in the actualization of faith, mutual trust becomes imperative. Trust demands disclosure and honesty among all parties. It implies openness to the other and a non-judgmental mind-set. This trust embraces not only the relationship between

[3] *The Code of Canon Law* restricts the term "ministry" to the clerical state. Yet subsequent to the promulgation of the code "ministry" has replaced the term "apostolate" and has become common parlance in speaking of the roles of the laity within the Church. Thus the non-canonical term will be used throughout this chapter.

[4] Canon law refers to those who are accountable for the juridic persons as "administrators." See canon 1279. However, the term "administrator" as commonly used, and as reflected in this chapter, refers to those who are entrusted with the day-to-day management of the ministry.

[5] See canon 675, §3.

the sponsors and the ministry but also the relationship of both with the official representatives of the Church itself.

Given the invariable premises of faith and trust, I suggest in addition five key expectations that sponsored ministries should anticipate from sponsors: unequivocal understanding of mission and vision, rootedness in charism and Catholic identity, clarity of roles, ongoing formation and support. These areas will be examined predominantly from the perspective of the sponsored ministry. However, since expectations entail communication and collaboration and because they imply a certain mutuality the sponsors' expectations of their ministries are also necessarily addressed.[6]

Mission and Vision

The sponsored ministry requires a clear understanding of its mission and vision. Those involved in governance and administration/management should expect to know how the sponsors propose to develop both in regard to the ministry. In order to share in the mission and to direct and to contribute to the vision, sponsored ministries need to perceive it from a perspective similar to the sponsors. Thus familiarity with the patrimony of the sponsors, i.e., possessing a sense of their history, charism and purpose, as well as understanding how the sponsored ministry is expected to foster this spirit is vital.[7] Trustees and administrators need to be familiar with the values that flow from the mission and how these are integrated into and lived out in the ministry. It is important that the sponsors communicate why the particular ministry started and equally essential for them to articulate why it continues. Those involved in the governance and administration of the sponsored ministry need to be conversant with this information. The sponsored ministry ought to be aware that it shares in and continues the mission of the sponsors and of the Church and that it stewards the patrimony of both. Those who serve on governing boards and as administrative leaders should appreciate their work as part of something greater than the particular ministry in which they serve and more encompassing than the sponsored entity itself.

[6] Much of what will be discussed in the five topics listed here is at times included in a sponsorship contract, agreement, or other written form that the sponsors share with those who work with them in leadership in the ministry.

[7] The concept of patrimony as used here is broad and interpreted in light of canon 578 that speaks of patrimony as constituting "the nature, purpose, spirit, and character of an institute" as well as its "sound traditions."

A further expectation in regard to the vision of the ministry is that those in leadership in the sponsored ministry be aware of future roles that might be open to the laity in light of their call to church ministry and the declining number of members in the sponsoring group. The implications of this reality will be further explored in the discussion of leadership formation.

CHARISM AND CATHOLIC IDENTITY

Sponsors, particularly those who are members of religious institutes, often devote significant time orienting and instructing sponsored ministries in regard to the charism of their community. Those in sponsored ministries need to be aware of the spirit that motivates the ministry, the spirit that they are entrusted to further through their participation in its particular work. This is accomplished in numerous ways: orientations, charism days, endowed chairs in fields relevant to the charism, pilgrimages to significant places connected with the founder/foundress, collaboration with the sponsors on issues of justice and stewardship, etc. Health care systems with multiple sponsors often strive to retain the charisms of the original founders as do other sponsored ministries even where no members of the sponsoring group are actually present.

Familiarity with the charism is important but even more so it is the role of the sponsors to make certain that those in the ministry are aware of the Catholic identity of the ministry. A recent study of Catholic colleges and universities, conducted by Melanie Morey and Dennis Holtschneider, suggests that those institutions that survive in the future will become less identified with a particular charism of a religious institute and more Catholic overall.[8] The study notes that exceptions to this could include religious groups whose charism is "familiar and hospitable to the laity." For the most part, however, a sense of the identity of the ministry will need to be deeply embedded in Catholic culture. This will enable the laity who govern, administer or serve in a particular institution to internalize its spirit and to be able to pass it on to those who succeed them. The authors of the study point out that memory in itself is inadequate in sustaining a culture. A charism requires a critical mass of

[8] Melanie Morey and Dennis Holtschneider, "Keeping the Faith on Campus," *Commonweal* 128 (April 20, 2001) 20-21. For a more in depth treatment of this topic see Melanie Morey and Dennis Holtschneider, "Relationship Revisited: Changing Relationships between US Catholic Colleges and Universities and Founding Religious Congregations," *Current Issues in Higher Education* 21(Fall 2000) 1-37, especially 31ff.

supporters to keep it alive. With high turnovers in education, health care, and social services it seems unlikely that smaller groups will be able to sustain their charism simply by sharing their story.[9]

Thus it is important to have a significant core of people within the sponsored ministry who can maintain and develop its Catholic identity. Ultimately all charisms are a reflection of the love of God as manifest in Jesus. It is the ministry of Jesus that continues in the works of sponsored entities regardless of the charism that mediates this.[10] Those who serve in sponsored ministries, particularly in governance and management roles, have a right to expect leadership from the sponsors in developing and strengthening the Catholic identity and culture of the ministry. Sponsors need to articulate the essential elements of Catholic identity that the ministry embraces. They should work with the sponsored ministry to assure that Christian inspiration permeates not only the individuals who minister within the institution but the institution itself. Sponsors must challenge the sponsored ministry to remain faithful to the Christian message as envisioned by the Church and to continue to contribute to the life and spirit of the Catholic faith through the works it performs. Sponsors must continually communicate the reality that the sharing of faith, which transcends and gives meaning to life, along with service to the people of God are foundational to the ministry.[11]

Those who serve in governance and on administrative teams of the sponsored ministry must be apprised of their leadership responsibility to support the Catholic character of the ministry. They should be cognizant of their

[9] Morey and Holtschneider, "Keeping the Faith on Campus," 21. The authors contend that it is unlikely that the plethora of Catholic subcultures (e.g., Apostles of the Sacred Heart, Marianites of the Holy Cross, Basilians, etc.) will be able to continue after members of those groups are no longer present in institutions. Groups that traditionally have attracted and embraced the laity in their charism, such as the Franciscans, might be able to sustain the founding group's identity in the future.

[10] David J. Nygren, "Effective Governance in Complex Systems," *Health Progress* (reprint) (July-August 2001) 24.

[11] John Paul II, Apostolic Constitution, *Ex corde Ecclesiae*, 15 August 1990, no. 13. The essential characteristics of Catholic identity are: "1. a strong inspiration not only of individuals but of the university community as such; 2. a continuing reflection in the light of the Catholic faith upon the growing treasury of human knowledge, to which it seeks to contribute by its own research; 3. fidelity to the Christian message as it comes to us through the Church; and 4. an institutional commitment to the service of the people of God and of the human family in their pilgrimage to the transcendent goal which gives meaning to life." Although the apostolic constitution relates these characteristics to Catholic education, these same principles can be adapted for other sponsored ministries.

responsibility to communicate this Catholic identity and all it implies to those who work in the ministry.[12] Leaders within the sponsored ministry must likewise be familiar with church law that frames and supports this identity. Trustees and senior managers of sponsored ministries need to understand that canon law is not simply supplementary to civil law; rather it is a primary vehicle that the Church employs to articulate, safeguard and promote the values that are inherent in its biblical and theological teachings. Those in leadership positions in sponsored ministries must realize that that they act in the name of the Church and are bound by all applicable church laws in administering the goods that belong to the juridic person.[13]

Clarity of Roles

Those who are involved in sponsored ministries, regardless of their position, need to be clear about their particular role in the ministry and the relationships that it involves. Sponsors, as well as those who serve on the governing board or in administrative leadership positions, require knowledge of the complexity of roles throughout the ministry. Whether the ministry is sponsored by a diocese, a religious institute or group of institutes, or is a public juridic person itself, each configuration of sponsorship requires role clarity. An examination of some of the more obvious relationships emphasizes this.

For the Sponsored Ministry

Sponsored ministries need to know the nature of their juridic person as well as they know the structure of the civil corporation of the entity. This entails a basic knowledge of church structure and canon law. Currently most church ministries share the public juridic personality of a diocese or a particular religious institute. However, this is not to be presumed as more frequently health care systems, universities and other entities are themselves becoming public juridic persons. There is also the possibility that a ministry could exist as or under the auspices of a private juridic person or an association of the faithful. Ministries that share in the juridic personality of religious institutes need to ascertain further whether the congregation is of diocesan or pontifical right and whether it is a province of a larger religious institute. Leaders in sponsored

[12] *Ex corde Ecclesiae*, Part II, Art. 4, §2.
[13] Robert Kennedy, "Temporal Goods of the Church" in *New Commentary on the Code of Canon Law*, ed. John Beal et al, (New York: Paulist Press, 2000) 1485.

ministries must know to whom they are accountable in regard to both the sponsor of the ministry and the Church and to whom they have recourse.

Those who share in the governance or administration of a sponsored ministry need to be aware of the authority their particular role grants them. Governing boards, which are civilly responsible for incorporated sponsored ministries, should be clear regarding what authority is reserved to the sponsors who represent the juridic person. Traditionally sponsors have reserved to themselves those powers that bear directly on the charter, mission, or philosophy of the institution; the approval of key leadership positions; decisions regarding leasing, selling, encumbering real estate in excess of a determined amount; and merging or dissolving the corporation.[14] However, sponsors may assume powers in addition to these traditional ones. Some sponsors, for example, reserve the right to conduct mission assessments in the sponsored ministry or the right to assure that certain positions, such as chair of the board or vice-president of mission, are held by members of the sponsoring religious institute or diocese. Sponsored ministries must know if they are expected to participate in business or stewardship practices similar to their sponsors in regard to advocacy or socially responsible investing. The sponsored entity has the right to expect full disclosure of such written or customary practices of the sponsor.[15]

Those in governance and administration in sponsored ministries should be familiar with the model of sponsorship employed. They need to know whether the sponsors are actively involved in the ministry or if they monitor it from a distance. Sponsored ministries require clarity regarding their accountability to the sponsors, and how this will be accomplished (through regularly scheduled meetings and/or by periodic written reports, etc.). They must be made aware of the sponsors' expectations of them and the means sponsors use to evaluate and assess their work in light of the mission of the ministry.

Likewise, those in leadership in sponsored ministries require clarity regarding their relationship to ecclesial authority. Sponsored ministries need to know that they are subject to visitation by the diocesan bishop who is responsible for all ministries within the diocese.[16] While the bishop is the administrator of diocesan ministries (although this role can be delegated), "religious are subject

[14] Reserved powers are typically derived from canon law concepts concerning a steward's ministry responsibilities. Reserved powers fulfill the canonical responsibilities and bridge together civil and canonical requirements.

[15] Many sponsors have a written sponsorship contract or agreement that describes the reserved powers as well as other expectations that exist between the sponsor and the ministry.

[16] See canon 397, §1. The visitation of the bishop is circumscribed in accord with his responsibility to exercise vigilance and coordination over the apostolates of the diocese. See also canon 394.

to the power of bishops...in those matters which regard...works of the apostolate."[17] Thus, the hospital/system CEO, the college president, or the agency director must know the parameters of her/his relationship with the bishop, whether this role is assumed by the sponsors or delegated to her/him, or mutually shared.

A final relationship in which sponsored ministries should expect clarification from the sponsor is the role of members of the sponsoring group who are employed by or who volunteer within the ministry. The presence of such individuals can be an asset, nonetheless their presence could also cause communication complications. While clergy/religious are members of the diocese/religious institute that sponsors the ministry, they themselves are not the actual sponsors. It is important for the sponsored ministry to know how these members are to be treated as employees. It could also be the case that one of the actual sponsors (i.e., one who is responsible for the juridic person) is employed by the ministry. In either case, roles and reporting relationships need to be clear to those entrusted with the administration of the sponsored ministry.

For the Sponsors

Sponsors need to be attentive to both the civil and the canonical implications of their sponsorship and to be able to communicate these clearly to sponsored ministries. This can be a challenge particularly when the members of the leadership team of a religious institute, by election, become the corporate member of sponsored ministries. Along with the learning curve required for the governance of the religious institute these new leaders need to gain knowledge of the workings of the sponsored ministries for which they are now responsible. Dialogue with the past leadership team and key resource persons, such as a sponsorship advisory committee, members who are knowledgeable about the sponsored ministries, lawyers or canonists, experts in health care, social work or education, can provide insight into the scope of their authority and how it has been traditionally exercised in the ministries. At the same time the leadership team's consciousness of its own strengths and style should be shared with the sponsored ministry.

Sponsors are required to be clear about their relationship to the president/CEO and to the board of trustees of the sponsored ministries. It is important for them to understand how local church authority perceives their

[17] Canon 678, §1.

role and to communicate with church leaders regarding what their role is with the sponsored ministry and who is its spokesperson.[18]

As far as possible sponsors need to educate the members of their community or group regarding the role of the sponsors. They need to assure that members of the sponsoring group know their status in the ministry as well as appropriate lines of communication and accountability.

Leadership Formation

Having examined expectations that the sponsored ministry should have of the sponsor in regard to mission and vision, charism and Catholic identity and clarity of roles, it is obvious that sponsors must provide leadership formation for those responsible for the governance and administration of the sponsored ministry. This is particularly imperative in light of the declining numbers of religious who currently sponsor a large percentage of U. S. church ministries. Morey and Holtschneider speak of the obligation of sponsors to "construct serious and sustained formative experiences for the lay people who will be in charge of [sponsored ministries]."[19] Likewise, Mary Kathryn Grant and Margaret Kopish point out that the formative responsibility of sponsors includes the added obligation of consciously identifying and forming "the next generation of sponsors."[20] John Paul II speaking of Catholic universities in *Ex corde Ecclesiae*, states that the future of Catholic higher education "depends to a great extent on the competent and dedicated service of lay Catholics." He recognizes "their developing presence in these institutions both as a sign of hope and as a confirmation of the irreplaceable lay vocation in the Church and in the world..."[21] The pope's words can equally apply to all the laity who share in governing or administering sponsored ministries other than education.

Thus sponsors need to assure that those in leadership roles in sponsored ministries receive a solid theological foundation. Those who minister in governance or administration in these entities can expect to build upon their faith experience. They should be versed in Catholic doctrine, spirituality, social teachings, morality and ethics and canon law as integral components of their

[18] As noted above religious are subject to the power of bishops in regard to apostolic works (c. 678, §1). The same canon in §3 speaks of the mutual consultation required of diocesan bishops and religious superiors in organizing works of the apostolate.

[19] Morey and Holtschneider, "Keeping the Faith on Campus," 23.

[20] See Mary Kathryn Grant and Margaret Kopish, ASC, "Sponsor Leadership Formation," *Health Progress* (July-August 2001) 26.

[21] *Ex corde Ecclesiae*, no. 25.

business operating practices. It is important for trustees and administrators to be comfortable with themselves as spiritual leaders as they in turn, become the conduits of the values of the ministry through their leadership of service to all who work within the sponsored entity. By way of analogy, as baptismal sponsors are entrusted with assisting and encouraging new Christians on their journey, so this same role should be expected of sponsors of ministries. As baptismal sponsors are eager to see the neophytes assume their rightful role in the ecclesial community, sponsors likewise should provide opportunities for developing both roots and wings for sponsored ministries.

Mary Kathryn Grant and Patricia Vandenberg in their book, *Partners in the Between Time*, take note of an evolution among those women and men who have ministered with religious in their sponsored works. They describe how in the early phases of sponsorship those assuming key administrative roles in the sponsored ministry question, "What do the sisters want?" As good sponsorship develops and lay leaders confidently grow in their role the question becomes, "What would the sisters do?" For those administrators who have solid theological and leadership formation and who are cognizant of and at home with their role in the sponsored ministry the question becomes, "What should we do?"[22]

This final query gains importance in regard to sponsorship in a society characterized by rapid change. Questions materialize in sponsored ministries that still need to be addressed by the Church. For instance, while canon law offers specifics about the acquisition, administration and alienation of property, it does not address the current issues regarding "partnerships, joint ventures, outreach initiatives, and other interwoven patterns of networking which blur the identity of Church ownership."[23] Yet these are ongoing issues for sponsors and for those who minister with them. Similarly, with unprecedented growth in technology and scientific advances, ethical issues arise that heretofore were non-existent. In such cases the sponsored ministry needs the expertise and guidance of the sponsors. Conversely, the sponsors rely on the skills of those in the sponsored ministry to respond creatively to these challenges in light of their theological foundation and professional expertise.

[22] Mary Kathryn Grant and Patricia Vandenberg, *Partners in the Between Time: Creating Sponsorship Capacity* (Michigan City, Indiana: Ministry Development Resources, 2004) 16-17.
[23] See Mary Kathryn Grant and Patricia Vandenberg, CSC, *After We're Gone: Creating Sustainable Sponsorship* (Mishawaka, Indiana: Ministry Development Resources, 1998) 116.

Support

It may appear superfluous at this point to state that sponsored ministries should look to sponsors for support. The topics previously discussed bear witness to this need. Yet there are other areas of assistance that the sponsored ministry has a right to expect from sponsors. Perhaps the most critical is open and ongoing dialogue. Sponsorship as an ever evolving commitment requires an open line of communication between the sponsors and the sponsored ministry. Those who govern or manage the ministry should know that they are truly *sponsored*. Sponsors need to challenge and evaluate sponsored ministries. They should be enthusiastic about and committed to the ministry that continues their legacy and the mission of the Church. Sponsors need to enter into strategic planning with their ministries, bringing their charismatic and prophetic voice to the table. At the same time they must be prepared to adapt their sponsorship for the good of the ministry. Sponsors need to see themselves not only as those who ultimately fulfill the canonical requirements of the ministry but more importantly as the leaven and spirit that animates it.

Those who work in leadership positions in sponsored ministries have voiced the need for sponsorship influence rather than control.[24] Sponsors are in the unique position to demonstrate that power is not necessarily best used in imposing demands but rather in the ability to motivate. By moving the hearts and stretching the imaginations of those entrusted with the governance and administration of the ministry, sponsors can affect positive change. Sponsors need to continue to explore creative ways of positively influencing sponsored ministries. Those ministering in sponsored entities should expect such inspiration and stimulus from their sponsors.

Although many religious institutes and dioceses involved in sponsorship are experiencing financial challenges themselves, sponsors should offer financial support when and where feasible. This can be done through annual appeals or capital campaigns or the donation of services or goods-in-kind to the sponsored ministry. Although the goal is that the sponsored ministry be financially solvent apart from the sponsors, nonetheless monetary contributions and gifts are symbolic of the supportive relationship that exists. On the other hand, sponsored ministries should support the sponsors where possible. While

[24] Morey and Holtschneider, "Keeping the Faith on Campus," 23.

sponsorship fees and/or annual donations might be offered to the sponsors by the sponsored ministry this is not a requirement.[25] Donations are gratuitous gifts exchanged between partners, not required obligations or debts.[26]

The presence of the sponsors and members of the sponsoring group within the ministry can be invaluable. The sponsors' presence at key events of the sponsored ministry symbolizes the mutuality that exists between them. Such experiences provide a strong visual expression of continuity and cohesiveness for those who work in the ministry and for those who are the beneficiaries of the service the ministry provides. Similarly the presence of members of the sponsoring groups who are employees or volunteers can accentuate the relationship between the sponsors and the sponsored ministry. These members have an opportunity to further the mission in a unique way. Their interaction with other employees in whatever capacity they serve demonstrates the reality of partnering in ministry. Yet physical presence in itself does not necessarily provide more impact. Members of the sponsoring group who are employees and volunteers should understand the role that they play, as should those involved in the governance and administration of the ministry.

As early as fifteen years ago Doris Gottemoeller, RSM addressed the possibility of religious communities continuing to sponsor ministries without members present in them. In such cases she observed that sponsors would have to be willing to put considerable effort into recruiting and preparing sisters for governance roles in these entities.[27] This rings even more true today. The sponsored ministry has a right to expect that sponsors and members of the sponsoring group who serve as members of the board or administrative team are knowledgeable and committed to their task. Other trustees/administrators should be able to look to such individuals for support and leadership particularly in regard to the mission and vision of the sponsoring group.

[25] It should be noted that sponsorship fee arrangements have civil law implications and need to be carefully executed with civil attorneys knowledgeable in this area.

[26] In a study of small Catholic colleges (Melanie Morey, *Leadership and Legacy: Is There a Future for the Past*, UMI Dissertation Services, Ann Arbor, MI 1995) 232, Morey notes that paradoxically "Congregational philanthropy plays an important role in the relationship between congregations and colleges…" While this might seem perplexing given the needs in many religious communities, Morey explains that her research shows that having been committed to principles of good stewardship many congregations are in a position to share their wealth with their ministries. She notes that "hospitals, schools, colleges and universities are recipients of these steward dollars" and that each of the colleges that she studied received annual substantial donations from their sponsoring group.

[27] See Doris Gottemoeller, "Institutions without Sisters," *Review for Religious*, 50 (July-August 1991) 567-568.

Those who serve in governance and administration in sponsored ministries may well have other expectations that are not dealt with in this chapter. It is important that valid expectations be shared with the sponsors. Trustees and administrators who see themselves working with rather than for the sponsors in regard to the mission of the institution are better prepared to experience the evolution of sponsorship. Those in sponsored ministries who see themselves fulfilling the mission of the Church in a corporate, rather than individual, manner through their work in sponsored ministries are better prepared to face the sponsorship issues that lie ahead.

Summation

Sponsorship in all its varied descriptions and models invites church members to a communal witness of the gospel. Those who choose to work in sponsored ministries in the Catholic Church necessarily participate to some degree in its public ministerial life. However, to many this prospect can be an experience that overwhelms or intimidates. Sponsorship at its best offers a mentoring-partnering relationship that encourages and supports lay leaders. It provides them with an experience of Church that is universal and all-inclusive. Sponsorship well executed enables the laity to develop theologically and to understand their rightful role in being and building Church.

Those in governance and administrative roles in sponsored ministries assume a co-responsible relationship with the sponsors. As such they need to express their expectations and hopes to the sponsors and to be open to the mutuality that these expectations demand. Trustees and administrators must embrace the mission and vision of the sponsors and integrate it into their lives and work. They need to be able to articulate the founding charism, live its values and give voice and witness to the Catholic identity of the institution. Lay leaders in sponsored ministries have the right to understand and the obligation to exercise their specific roles and to be clear about the requirements that are theirs from a Church perspective. Their role demands ongoing formation and a reliance on the support of those who are their sponsors.

Undergirding all these expectations is the fundamental truth that those in sponsored ministries must share a mutual faith and trust with those who sponsor. The relationship between sponsors and sponsored ministries will continue to evolve; both are responsible for continuing, directing and encouraging the mission of Jesus manifest in the world today through their particular ministry.

CONCLUSION

Learnings And Future Possibilities

As the chapters of this study have indicated, the topic of sponsorship is indeed a complex one. Each of our distinguished authors has addressed one aspect of the total picture of the dynamic and multi-faceted reality known as sponsorship. Readers – canonists and civil attorneys, bishops and major superiors, religious and lay leaders who make the diverse sponsored ministries effective vehicles of God's compassion and service in our world – all have their own stories to tell and experiences to share about how the sponsorship relation works. It is hoped that the contributions in this study provide helpful information and insights to our readers regarding the purposes and structures, benefits and challenges of this life-giving relationship known as sponsorship. If real exchange and learning occur, this work will have accomplished its purpose.

The Term Sponsorship

As noted in the Introduction to this book and echoed by several of the contributors, the word "sponsorship" is not defined per se in either canon law or civil law. For the purposes of this study the following common working definition was developed indicating the basic components of the concept:

> *Sponsorship of an apostolate or ministry is a formal relationship between a recognized Catholic organization and a legally formed entity, entered into for the sake of promoting and sustaining the Church's mission in the world.*

This generic definition both assumes and suggests that the relationships being defined are diverse, unpredictable, evolutionary and ambiguous, with little formal canonical or civil legal anchor. Sponsorship is an evolving reality, and canon law can attempt to guide its evolving structures using basic legal principles while testing the relationships in praxis. The terms "sponsored institutions", "sponsored ministries" or simply "congregational ministries" are often used interchangeably and are, for that reason, inherently imprecise. In general, canonists would urge more precision, but some would ask if the Church has had enough experience with sponsorship to develop a firm and consistent lexicon. It is agreed, however, that the language used to describe sponsorship relationships must be disciplined, especially if transferred to any civil legal documents.

In the papers of this study, the primary reference point of the authors is sponsorship in relation to the ministries of education and health care. Social services might also have been included, as the principles are the same even though the applications vary. However, many social service organizations affiliated with Catholic sponsors appear to have even greater diversity than those of education or health care, and it becomes more difficult to describe general types, structures and relationships. Perhaps as the ministries of education and healthcare continue to migrate from their traditional institutional bases there will be some mutual transfer of knowledge and experience.

Traditionally, religious institutes have constituted the major portion of the sponsors for the apostolates within the Catholic community. Religious institutes, by their very nature charismatic and entrepreneurial, will continue to evolve and develop side by side with the institutional presence of their sponsored ministries. Vital religious institutes will continue their entrepreneurial spirit providing ministry in response to needs, and these ministries may not fit neatly into the current understandings of sponsorship. Moreover, some of these emerging ministries may take the form of the work of an individual religious, carried on for a given time with the blessing of the superior. On the other hand, the new work may simply be a ministry to which the religious institute contributes financial support without any other ties or responsibilities.

As more dioceses and/or parishes begin to assume or expand oversight responsibility for particular ministries such as healthcare services and educational institutions, the experience which religious institutes have had with sponsorship can serve as models or, at the very least, as sources of wisdom. In many ways the civil and canonical structures currently developing may be similar to those of the past, with the diocesan bishop or pastor holding authority and exercising leadership in these ministries similar to that held and experienced by the religious superior for the religious institute's ministries. Both diocesan canonists and civil lawyers could benefit from the experience religious institutes have accrued over the last 200 years.

LEARNINGS

While each paper in this study has been focused on one particular facet of sponsorship and explored avenues specific to that topic, some overarching questions and learnings emerge. We gather some of these fragments together and pose some general learnings and observations as a contribution to the ongoing discussion.

First, the declining number of priests and religious available for leadership roles both in the sponsored ministries and in the religious institute itself underlines the need for greater clarity in the description of sponsorship relationships. More formal clarification is a proactive exercise of stewardship and discussion regarding mutual expectations for the sponsorship relationship in each ministry or institution sets the stage for productive exchange.

Second, this same decline in the number of clergy and religious suggests a need for greater collaboration between and among similar institutions. Structures to formalize and 'institutionalize' such collaboration tend be more complex than those involving a single institution and/or single sponsor. In addition, as lay people, many of whom may have no connection to any of the original founding religious institutions, assume more leadership roles in these collaborative ventures, greater intentionality in sharing mission and charism as well as greater clarification regarding structures, expectations and limits will be essential.

Third, one learning which has surfaced repeatedly is the need to identify and empower a member of senior management to focus on the mission of the sponsored ministry. The importance of this role is exacerbated by the declining number of religious and clergy active in the sponsored ministry, persons who in previous eras embodied the mission implicitly but concretely. The mission integration position at the highest level of the organization assists with leadership development and deeper reflection of the mission, raises questions and helps ground decision-making in the coordinates of purpose and charism. The position of mission leader, whether filled by a religious or a lay person, must be sufficiently senior in the organization for it to be effective.

Fourth, since both religious institutes and their sponsored ministries are church entities, the physical goods and property pertaining therewith need to be tracked carefully, identifying what belongs to the religious institute itself and what belongs to the ministry. Further, it is important to distinguish between what is 'patrimony', and therefore stable and not to be disposed of, and what has not been stabilized and therefore may be used in various ways.

A written inventory, whether taken at the time of the foundation of the sponsored ministry, decades after the foundation or just as a new sponsorship relationship unfolds, helps determine both for the present and the future what must be retained and what may be disposed of. Those goods designated as stable patrimony must be used for and directed to either the religious institute or the apostolic purpose for which they have been designated as patrimony.

Fifth, the Catholic Church and its canon law have a role to play in guiding church-related organizations as they develop their civil law structures. At either the original incorporation or upon a subsequent restructuring of a ministry of the Church, those civil law structures should be used which best serve the purposes of the church and of the particular ministry. For sponsored ministries, the ecclesial purpose and mission must take precedence over other purposes. Aware of the importance of structures for the long term, care must be taken regarding preservation and use of all civil documents.

Sixth, much current practice in the area of sponsorship depends on the interaction between the powers held/exercised by the Board of Trustees of the civilly incorporated entity and those powers reserved by law to the Member corporation, usually populated by the major superior and council. In addition, from time to time the Member corporation, again through the major superior, may delegate certain other of its powers to the Board. The content of this delegation depends on many factors, including specific circumstances of the ministry, competing demands, and/or the particular skill set or interests of the major superior. When a particular major superior's term ends and another major superior, perhaps with a different perspective and expectations, assumes office, the delegated powers may change. Understandably such give-and-take can be unsettling to a Board, which may feel as if building on shifting sand. Consistency, continuity and predictability make for greater stability in the sponsorship relationship and in the actual governance oversight of the institution. In all cases, the content and duration of any delegation of powers should be committed to writing.

Lastly, most canonists acknowledge the historical nature of the Church's canon law and how it has evolved gradually over centuries borrowing heavily from Roman law, and arriving at its present formulation. Most canonists also acknowledge that canon law continues to develop as new situations demand new responses. In certain areas it is evident that the canon law needs to be clearer and perhaps more flexible to support and facilitate emerging sponsorship structures. As noted in the study itself, two areas where further canonical development might better serve this developing area of sponsorship include greater clarity in the distinction between private and public juridic persons and further exploration of private associations.

CONCLUDING THOUGHT

Finally, given the rapid development of sponsorship structures and the diminishment in membership of the religious institutes which founded them, it becomes imperative that the whole church share responsibility for ministries once established and run by religious institutions. This broader ecclesial responsibility includes providing resources to prepare lay leaders to assume leadership in these and other ministries of the church.

Sponsorship offers a rich but complex vehicle through which to carry forward the mission of Christ. As new possibilities present themselves the sponsorship relationship will continue to evolve. Canonists and those who work with them in shaping the ministry for the future must be able to adapt to changing needs, maintaining what is core and creatively facilitating the emergence of the new.

Selected Bibliography

Catholic Health Association of the United States. *Sponsorship: Resources for Sponsors.* St. Louis, MO: Catholic Health Association, 2005.

________. *The Search for Identity: Canonical Sponsorship of Catholic Healthcare.* St. Louis, MO: Catholic Health Association, 1993.

Coborn, Carol K., and Martha Smith. *Spirited Lives: How Nuns Shaped Catholic Culture and American Life, 1836-1920.* Chapel Hill, NC: The University of North Carolina Press, 1999.

Conlin, Daniel C. "Sponsorship at the Crossroads." *Health Progress* 82 (July-August 2001): 20-23.

________. "The McGrath Thesis and its Impact on a Canonical Understanding of the Ownership of Ecclesiastical Goods." *CLSA Proceedings* 64 (2002): 73-96.

Conn, James J. "Catholic Universities in the United States and Ecclesiastical Authority". *Analecta Gregoriana* 259. Rome: Editrice Pontificia Università Gregoriana, 1991.

________. "Bishops and the Apostolates of Religious." *CLSA Proceedings* 63 (2001): 49-83.

Deacon, Florence. "Handmaids or Autonomous Women: The Charitable Activities, Institution Building and Communal Relationships of Catholic Sisters in Nineteenth Century Wisconsin". Ph.D diss., The University of Wisconsin-Madison, 1989.

DePaolis, V. "The Temporal Goods of the Church in the New Code with Particular Reference to Institutes of Consecrated Life." *The Jurist* 43 (1983): 343-360.

DiPietro, Melanie. "Changes in Governance of Catholic Colleges and Universities: Some Practical Observations." *Current Issues in Catholic Higher Education* 11 (Winter, 1991): 8-13.

_______. "Impact of Canon Law on Health Care Delivery." *Hospital Contract Manual*, vol. 3. Edited by Baker Hosteller and Robert Wolin. Gaithersburg, MD: Aspen Publishers, 2000.

_______. "Incorporated Apostolates." *Church Finance Handbook*. Edited by Kevin McKenna, Lawrence DiNardo and Joseph Pokusa. Washington, DC: Canon Law Society of America, 1999: 279-303.

_______. "The Interfacing of Canonical Principles and American Law in the Negotiation of Joint Ventures Between Church-Related and Non-Church-Related Corporations." *Acts of the Colloquium: Public Ecclesiastical Juridic Persons and Their Apostolates in the Catholic Church in the USA: Canonical-Civil Aspects.* Rome: Pontifical University of Saint Thomas Aquinas, 1998.

Dolan, Jay P. *The American Catholic Experience.* Garden City, NY: Doubleday, 1985.

Drahmann, Theodore. "Sponsorship." *Current Issues in Catholic Higher Education* 11 (Winter, 1991): 26-27.

Ewens, Mary. *The Role of the Nun in 19th Century America.* Salem, NH: Ayer, 1984.

Fialka, John J. *Sisters: Catholic Nuns and the Making of America.* New York: St. Martin's Press, 2003.

Fox, Joseph. "Introductory Thoughts about Public Juridic Persons and their Civilly Incorporated Apostolates." *Angelicum* 76 (1999): 583-613.

Furay, Sally M. "Preserving the Mission into the Future." *Current Issues in Catholic Higher Education* 23 (Summer, 2003): 51-60.

Gallin, Alice. *Independence and a New Partnership in Catholic Higher Education.* Notre Dame, IN: University of Notre Dame Press, 1996.

_______. *Negotiating Identity.* Notre Dame, IN: University of Notre Dame Press, 2000.

_______. *American Catholic Higher Education: Essential Documents, 1967-1990.* Notre Dame, IN: University of Notre Dame Press, 1992.

_______. "On the Road Toward a Definition of a Catholic University." *The Jurist* 48 (1988): 536-558.

Gibbons, Robert. "Sponsors and Directors: An Important Conversation." *Current Issues in Catholic Higher Education* 11 (Winter, 1991): 23-25.

Grant, Mary Kathryn. "Exercising Sponsorship: Five Essential Tasks." *Current Issues in Catholic Higher Education* 23 (Summer, 2003): 61-66.

________. "'Reframing' Sponsorship." *Health Progress* 82 (July-August 2001): 38-40.

Grant, Mary Kathryn, and Patricia Vandenberg. *After We're Gone: Creating Sustainable Sponsorship*. Mishawaka, IN: Ministry Development Resources, 1998.

________. *Partners in the Between Time: Creating Sponsorship Capacity*. Mishawaka, IN: Ministry Development Resources, 2004.

Gray, Katherine. "New Sponsorship Model Responds to Needs." *Health Progress* 86 (January-February 2005): 51-52.

Harrington, Peter. "Civil and Canon Law Issues Affecting American Catholic Higher Education 1948-1998: An Overview and the ACCU Perspective." *Current Issues in Catholic Higher Education* 20 (Fall, 1999): 45-87.

Hesburgh, Theodore M. (ed). *The Challenge and Promise of a Catholic University* Notre Dame, IN: University of Notre Dame Press, 1994.

Hite, Jordan. *A Primer on Public and Private Juridic Persons: Applications to the Healthcare Ministry*. St. Louis, MO: Catholic Health Association, 2000.

Holland, Sharon. "Sponsorship and the Vatican." *Health Progress* 82 (July-August 2001): 32-37, 52.

John Paul II. apostolic constitution *Ex corde Ecclesiae*. August 15, 1990. *Origins* 20 (October 4, 1990): 265, 267-276.

Keiss, Isabelle. "The Relationship Between an Institution's Trustees and Its Sponsoring Religious Community." *Current Issues in Catholic Higher Education* 11 (Winter1991): 28-30.

Kennedy, Robert. "McGrath, Maida, Michiels: Introduction to a Study of the Canonical and Civil-Law Status of Church-Related Institutions in the United States." *The Jurist* 50 (1990): 351-401.

King, William J. "The Corporation Sole and Subsidiarity." *CLSA Proceedings* 65 (2003): 107-134.

Langan, John P. (ed). *Catholic Universities in Church and Society*. Washington, DC: Georgetown University Press, 1993.

Lee, Bernard L. "Charism as Culture: Congregational Sponsorship of Colleges and Universities." *Current Issues in Catholic Higher Education* 23 (Summer, 2003): 45-50.

Maida, Adam. *Ownership, Control and Sponsorship of Catholic Institutions: A Practical Guide*. Harrisburg, PA: Pennsylvania Catholic Conference, 1975.

Maida, Adam, and Nicholas Cafardi. *Church Property, Church Finances and Church Related Corporations.* St. Louis: Catholic Health Association of the United States, 1984.

Manny, J. "Governance Issues for Non-Profit Religious Organizations." *The Catholic Lawyer* 40/1 (2000): 1-22.

McGrath, John J. *Catholic Institutions in the United States: Canonical and Civil Law Status.* Washington, DC: The Catholic University of America Press, 1968.

Moots, Philip and Edward Gaffney, eds. *Church and Campus: Legal Issues in Religiously Affiliated Higher Education.* Notre Dame, IN: University of Notre Dame Press, 1979.

Morey, Melanie and Dennis Holtschneider. "Relationship Revisited: Changing Relationships Between U.S. Catholic Colleges and Universities and Founding Religious Congregations." *Current Issues in Catholic Higher Education* 21 (Fall, 2000): 3-39.

Morrisey, Francis G. "Catholic Identity in a Challenging Environment." *Health Progress* 80 (1999): 38-42.

________ . Improving the Identity of Catholic Health Care Institutions' Structures." *Dolentium Hominum* 18 (2003): 128-134. (Pontifical Council for Health Pastoral Care)

________."Toward Juridic Personality." *Health Progress* 82 (July-August 2001): 27-31, 51.

________. "Trustees and Canon Law." *Health Progress* 83 (November-December 2002): 11-18.

Nygren, David. "Effective Governance in Complex Systems." *Health Progress* 82 (July-August 2001): 41-45.

O'Brien, David J. *From the Heart of the American Church.* Maryknoll, NY: Orbis Books, 1994.

Peter, Sean, Barbara Conroy, Marcia Lunz, Mary Mollison and Anne Munley. "Beyond the Present: The Shape of Sponsorship in the 21st Century." *Current Issues in Catholic Higher Education* 23 (Summer 2003): 67-75.

Place, Michael. "Toward a Theology of Sponsorship." *Health Progress* 85 (January-February, 2004): 6-9.

Power, Edward J. *A History of Catholic Higher Education in the United States.* Milwaukee: The Bruce Publishing Company, 1958.

Provost, James. "The Sides of Catholic Identity." *Current Issues in Catholic Higher Education* 14 (Winter 1994): 16-19.

Savage, Thomas. "Trustees and Sponsors of Catholic Higher Education: What Should They be Talking About Together?" *Current Issues in Catholic Higher Education* 11 (Winter 1991): 5-7.

Schmidt, J.R. "Review of 'Catholic Institutions in the United States: Canonical and Civil Status', by J. J. McGrath." *The Jurist* 28 (1968): 228-235.

Stamm, Martin. "Emerging Corporate Models of Governance in Contemporary American Catholic Higher Education." *Current Issues in Catholic Higher Education* 2 (Summer 1981): 38-45.

Stepsis, Ursula, and Dolores Liptak, ed. *Pioneer Healers.* New York: Crossroads, 1989.

United States Conference of Catholic Bishops. *Guidelines Concerning the Academic Mandatum in Catholic Universities.* Washington, DC: USCCB, 2001.

________. *Ethical and Religious Directives for Catholic Health Care Services.* Washington, DC: USCCB, 2001.

________. *The Application of Ex corde Ecclesiae for the Untied States. Origins* 30 (June 15, 2000): 68-75.

Warner, Richard. "The Relationship Between Trustees and Sponsoring Religious Congregations." *Current Issues in Catholic Higher Education* 11 (Winter 1991): 14-16.

West, A. "Legal Status and Administrative Control of Religious Organizations and Groups in France." *The Catholic Lawyer* 33 (1988): 285-304.

Wilson, Charles. "Catholic Colleges and Civil Law: Benefits and Burden of Government Involvement in Higher Education." *Current Issues in Catholic Higher Education* 17 (Fall 1997): 3, 39-49.

Contributors

BEAL, John P.

John Beal is a presbyter of the Diocese of Erie, Pennsylvania. He received his doctorate in canon law from The Catholic University of America in 1985 and is currently professor of canon law there. He is co-editor of and contributor to *A New Commentary on the Code of Canon Law* and has published many articles in a variety of journals.

BROWN, Warren A., OMI

Warren Brown is a priest of the Missionary Oblates of Mary Immaculate and serves as provincial councilor at large of the U.S. Oblate Province. He earned a doctorate in canon law from Saint Paul University, Ottawa. Presently, he is executive vice president and assistant professor of canon law, Oblate School of Theology, San Antonio. He has experience in the marriage tribunal and serves as the judicial vicar of the Appellate Tribunal for the Arch/Dioceses of Texas.

BURNS, Helen Marie, RSM

Helen Marie Burns recently completed a six-year term on the Institute Leadership Team for the Sisters of Mercy of the Americas. She has served in various leadership roles within her religious congregation for the past twenty-five years and was elected to the Presidency of the Leadership Conference of Women Religious in 1988. Helen Marie holds a masters degree in English from the University of Wisconsin and a doctoral degree from the School of Religion, University of Iowa. She has lectured extensively on the topics of religious life, leadership, sponsorship and the charism and tradition of the Sisters of Mercy. She has also published several articles on these topics.

DIPIETRO, Sister Melanie, SC

Melanie DiPietro, a Sister of Charity of Seton Hill, Greensburg, Pennsylvania, is a member with the law firm of Buchanan Ingersoll PC. She concentrates her practice representing religious and church-related public charitable corporations in governance and transactional matters. Melanie is also the 2005-2006

Distinguished Practitioner in Residence at Seton Hall Law School and serves as an elected member of the American Law Institute and on the Members Consultant Group on the Principles of Nonprofit Corporations. She holds a law degree from Duquesne University and a doctorate in canon law from the Pontifical University of Saint Thomas Aquinas in Rome.

DUGAN, Patricia M.

Patricia Dugan, a lay person, holds a degree in civil law from the Villanova University Law School in Pennsylvania. She received her licentiate in canon law from the Pontifical University of Saint Thomas Aquinas in Rome, and her Masters in Religious Studies from Saint Charles Seminary in Philadelphia, PA. She maintains practices in both legal systems in Philadelphia. Her published works deal with Church finances and penal proceedings.

GOLDEN, Paul L., CM

Paul Golden is the director of Vincentian Canonical Services in Denver, CO. A Vincentian priest, he has been teaching canon law since 1968. He served as Rector/President of St. Thomas Theological Seminary in Denver, Vice President of DePaul University in Chicago and President of Niagara University in Niagara, NY. Paul has also served as President of the Canon Law Society of America.

HOLLAND, Sharon L., IHM

Sharon Holland, a member of the Sisters, Servants of the Immaculate Heart of Mary of Monroe, MI, is on the staff of the Congregation for Institutes of Consecrated Life and Societies of Apostolic Life in Rome and teaches canon law at the Pontifical Institute Regina Mundi. She received a doctorate in canon law from the Gregorian University and has been a contributor to a number of CLSA publications.

KING, William J.

William King is a priest of the Diocese of Harrisburg, currently on loan to the Archdiocese of Atlanta, where he serves as Judicial Vicar. He is also Promoter of Justice of the Maronite Eparchy of Saint Maron, adjunct Instructor in Canon Law at The Catholic University of America, and has served on the Board of Governors of the Canon Law Society of America and as chair of several of its committees. He earned a Licentiate in Canon Law at The Catholic University of America in 1989, and Doctorate of Canon Law at the Pontifical Gregorian University in 2002.

MORRISEY, Francis, OMI

Francis Morrisey was ordained to the priesthood in 1961 in the Congregation of the Oblates of Mary Immaculate. He holds an M.A., a Ph.L., a S.T.L. and Doctorate in Canon Law, received in 1971. Currently He is a Professor of Canon Law at Saint Paul University in Ottawa, Canada. Frank is a former Dean of the Faculty at Saint Paul University (1972-1984) and author of numerous studies relating to sponsorship, health care and Church finances.

REYNOLDS, Nancy, SP

Nancy Reynolds is a member of the Sisters of Providence of Saint Mary-of-the-Woods, Indiana. She obtained her licentiate in canon law from The Catholic University of America in 1984. She practiced canon law in tribunal ministry for 24 years, taught canon law in several schools of theology and in various master's programs. She is presently a member of her Congregation's General Council.

SMITH, Patricia, OSF

Patricia Smith, is a member of the Sisters of St. Francis of Philadelphia. She received her doctoral degree in canon law from Saint Paul University and has worked in the area of sponsorship for her community and as a consultant. Presently she teaches canon law at the University of Notre Dame, South Bend, IN during the fall semester and theology and Franciscan studies at Neumann College, Aston, PA in the spring semester.

SMITH, Rosemary, SC

Rosemary Smith, a Sister of Charity of Saint Elizabeth, is Senior Vice President, Sponsorship with Bon Secours Health System in Virginia. Rosemary has served in a variety of ministries, including professor of Canon Law at St. Mary Seminary in Houston, Texas; judge in diocesan tribunals; canonical consultant to religious institutes; and in leadership in her own religious congregation. She has published numerous articles in the field of canon law. Rosemary earned her doctorate in canon law at The Catholic University of America.